PEARSON
REALITY CENTRAL
Readings in the Real World

PEARSON

Upper Saddle River, New Jersey • Boston, Massachusetts
Chandler, Arizona • Glenview, Illinois • Shoreview, Minnesota

TABLE OF CONTENTS

 Unit 1 BQ: Is truth the same for everyone?

TABLE OF CONTENTS

 Unit 2 BQ: Can all conflicts be resolved?

Unit 3 BQ: How much information is enough?

TABLE OF CONTENTS

 Unit 4 BQ: What is the secret to reaching someone with words?

Unit 5 BQ: Is it our differences or our similarities that matter most?

TABLE OF CONTENTS

Unit 6 BQ: Are yesterday's heroes important today?

ABOUT YOUR BOOK

The What and Why of this Book

This book is a collection of articles written with you in mind. The articles are on real-life topics you and your friends might talk about. In fact, you may even disagree about them. This is because the topics often have two or more sides.

The Big Question

The articles in this book are broken down into units. Each unit has a Big Question like this one: **How do we decide what is true?** After you read the articles in a unit, you will use them to answer the Unit Big Question. Each article also has its own main question for you to think about as you read. This question connects the article to the Unit BQ.

Unit Opener

Each unit begins with an opener that shows a real-life situation and connects to the Unit BQ. Use the opener to prepare for the unit articles.

The Big Question
Here is the Unit Big Question.

Introduction
This paragraph connects you to the situation shown in the art.

Prompt
Use this question to put yourself into the situation pictured.

Kick It Off

Before each article you will find a Kick It Off page. This page will help you get ready to read the article.

Real-Life Connection
Use this section to think about the article topic. Here you may also see a graphic organizer to help you collect ideas.

Check It Out
This section provides important information on the article topic if you need more background.

Word Bank
Here are words that are important in the article. Notice that they are bold.

KICK IT OFF — Leveling the Playing Field

Real-Life Connection
Belinda grew up playing football with her older brothers, and she is an excellent player. She wants to try out for the high school football team, but football is a boys' sport. Take a moment to write your thoughts on the pros and cons of Belinda playing high school football.

Check It Out
Title IX (referred to as "Title Nine") is a law that was passed in the United States in 1972 to ensure girls had equal opportunities in sports. This law allows girls to play on boys' teams in schools in which there are no girls' teams in the same sports.

- Title IX works for boys, too. If they want to compete in a sport that is offered only for girls, they can try out for the girls' team.
- Title IX also makes sure other educational opportunities are equal for boys and girls.

WORD BANK

bias (BY uhs) *noun*   To have a **bias** means to prefer one group or one thing over another every time.

The Article

These short articles are like the ones you might read in magazines or on-line. Before you read, look for these features to get you started:

Unit Big Question
The Unit Big Question is repeated here to help you remember.

Article
Now the article begins. Do not forget to read the title!

THE BIG ?
Is truth the same for everyone?
A girl kicks the winning field goal for her school football team. Another girl pins her opponent in a wrestling match. Events like these might surprise you, but there is a good chance they are happening in your town right now. As you read the article, ask yourself: Should girls be allowed to play on boys' sports teams?

Leveling the Playing Field

"**O**bviously, boys are better at just about everything. It's just natural," says a student on a sports blog. Is this **opinion** correct? Are boys better at sports than girls are? Should only boys play certain sports?

Until thirty-five years ago, girls did not have a chance to play all of the sports that boys played. Most high schools and colleges had a **bias** toward traditionally male sports like football, basketball, baseball, and wrestling. There were fewer girls' sports offered at most schools. In addition, most schools

Article Big Question
Use this section to connect to the Article Big Question in blue.

Read the Article

As you read the article you will notice several tools. These tools are here to help explain the article and to keep information organized and clear.

Vocabulary
Word banks terms and their forms are set bold to help you collect ideas.

Subheads
Subheads help you preview what this section of the article will be about.

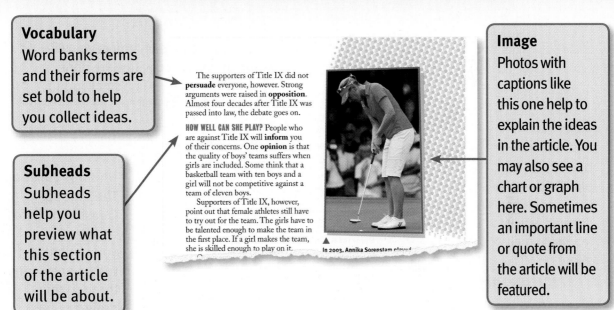

The supporters of Title IX did not **persuade** everyone, however. Strong arguments were raised in **opposition**. Almost four decades after Title IX was passed into law, the debate goes on.

HOW WELL CAN SHE PLAY? People who are against Title IX will **inform** you of their concerns. One **opinion** is that the quality of boys' teams suffers when girls are included. Some think that a basketball team with ten boys and a girl will not be competitive against a team of eleven boys.

Supporters of Title IX, however, point out that female athletes still have to try out for the team. The girls have to be talented enough to make the team in the first place. If a girl makes the team, she is skilled enough to play on it.

In 2003, Annika Sorenstam played

Image
Photos with captions like this one help to explain the ideas in the article. You may also see a chart or graph here. Sometimes an important line or quote from the article will be featured.

Wrap It Up

After each article you will find a Wrap It Up box. This section is here to help you check your understanding and summarize what you have learned.

Find It on the Page
The answers to these questions can be found in the article.

Use Clues
You will have to use clues from the article and your own thinking to answer these questions.

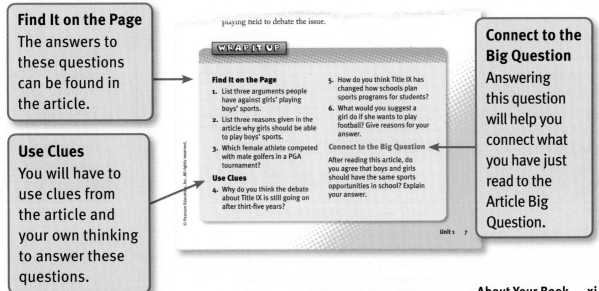

playing field to debate the issue.

WRAP IT UP

Find It on the Page

1. List three arguments people have against girls' playing boys' sports.

2. List three reasons given in the article why girls should be able to play boys' sports.

3. Which female athlete competed with male golfers in a PGA tournament?

Use Clues

4. Why do you think the debate about Title IX is still going on after thirt-five years?

5. How do you think Title IX has changed how schools plan sports programs for students?

6. What would you suggest a girl do if she wants to play football? Give reasons for your answer.

Connect to the Big Question

After reading this article, do you agree that boys and girls should have the same sports opportunities in school? Explain your answer.

Connect to the Big Question
Answering this question will help you connect what you have just read to the Article Big Question.

Unit Wrap Up

At the end of each unit you will find a fun project that will help you put everything you read together to answer the Unit Big Question.

Page 1

Project
This is the type of project you will be doing. All activities are done with a partner or in a small group.

Unit Articles
Use this list to pick articles that you especially enjoyed or want to think more about.

UNIT 1 WRAP UP

PROJECT: Write-Around

Answer the Big Question: Is truth the same for everyone?
You have read about issues that center on truth. Now, use what you learned to answer the Unit 1 Big Question (BQ).

UNIT 1 ARTICLES

Leveling the Playing Field, pp. 8–11

Separate Justice, pp. 4–7

This Land Is Whose Land? pp. 12–15

Laws That Work for Kids Who Work, pp. 16–19

Debating the Ratings, pp. 24–27

STEP 1: Form a Group and Choose
Your first step is to pick Unit 1 articles that you like.
Get together. Find a small group to work with.
Read the list of articles. Discuss which articles listed on the left side of this page were the most interesting to you.
Choose two or more articles. Pick articles that you all agree on.

STEP 2: Reread and Answer the Unit Big Question
Your next step is to answer the Unit BQ in your group.
Reread the articles you chose. As you reread, think about the Unit BQ.
Answer questions. For each article you chose, answer these questions:
• What is the topic, or central issue, of this article?

Unit Big Question
The Unit Big Question is listed here to remind you of what you will be answering through this project.

Page 2

...pport

...ize the write-around. Be sure that viewpoints are supported with reasons. Choose the reasons that are most convincing. Remember, a summary includes the most important ideas—not all the ideas.

STEP 5: Check and Fix
Next, you and your group will look over your write-around summary to see if it could be improved.
Use the rubric. Use the questions to evaluate your work. Answer each question yes or no. If you would like another opinion about your summary, trade with another group and use the rubric again.
Discuss your evaluations. For your yes answers, think about what you can do to strengthen your summary. If you have any no answers, talk about what you can do to turn each no into a yes.
Improve your summary. After discussing the results of using the rubric, work together to make your summary stronger.

STEP 6: Practice and Present
Get ready to present your write-around and summary to classmates.
Practice what you want to say. You will use your write-around to explain your group's answer to the Unit BQ. You might have each group member present his or her answer. Then a group spokesperson might present the summary.
Present your work. Explain your an... ...your classmates. In a ...

RUBRIC

Does the summary . . .
• answer the Unit BQ?
• include details from at least two articles in Unit 1?
• show a clear relationship between the answer and the reasons given to support it?
• include the viewpoints of all group members, even if group members disagreed?
• show a clear organization by starting with the answer to the Unit BQ and then supporting that answer with details?

Activity Steps
Steps are numbered with helpful directions and questions to walk you through the project.

Rubric
Use the rubric to make sure you have included all the important information in your project.

Textbook Scavenger Hunt

To make the most of independent learning, you will need to use the unique features of this book on your own. Now that you have reviewed the features of this text, use this scavenger hunt to get to know your book from cover to cover.

With a partner or small group answer the questions below on your own paper. Use the walk-through on the previous pages as a quick reminder if you need it. Then share your responses with the class.

1 Turn to the Table of Contents. Scan to find an article that interests you. How can you find the article in the book? Turn to the article. What question will you answer as you read?

2 How are the topics in the index organized? Scan the index to find a topic that interests you. Then flip to an article that covers this topic. What do the captions, illustrations, and other visuals tell you about the article?

3 How many units are in the book? How can you tell? Flip through your book. Pause at the unit opener illustration you like best. How does it help you connect to the Unit Big Question?

4 Where will you find a Real-Life Connection with each article? Find one that includes a graphic organizer. What information will the graphic organizer help you to think about and organize?

5 What do the special quote features in this book look like? Find an article that features a quote. What information about the article does the quote give you?

6 Locate the glossary. Find a word that you do not know and share the definition with a friend. What other information about the word can you find in the glossary?

Is truth the same for everyone?

The player and the umpire saw the same play, yet their beliefs about it are very different. In this unit, you will read about other issues that make people disagree. You will think about what is or is not true, and you will figure out what *you* think about the Big Question.

Recall a time when you and a friend disagreed about music or a movie. Why did you disagree? Was one of you right, or were you both "right"? Explain.

Real-Life Connection

Belinda grew up playing football with her older brothers, and she is an excellent player. She wants to try out for the high school football team, but football is a boys' sport. Take a moment to write your thoughts on the pros and cons of Belinda playing high school football.

Check It Out

Title IX (referred to as "Title Nine") is a law that was passed in the United States in 1972 to ensure girls had equal opportunities in sports. This law allows girls to play on boys' teams in schools in which there are no girls' teams in the same sports.

- Title IX works for boys, too. If they want to compete in a sport that is offered only for girls, they can try out for the girls' team.
- Title IX also makes sure other educational opportunities are equal for boys and girls.

WORD BANK

bias (BY uhs) *noun*   To have a **bias** means to prefer one group or one thing over another every time.
EXAMPLE: *Miles admits he has a **bias** against people owning pit bulls.*

inform (in FAWRM) *verb*   When you **inform** someone of something, you give the person knowledge of it.
EXAMPLE: *The bus driver had to **inform** the kids of the rules.*

opinion (uh PIN yuhn) *verb*   An **opinion** is the way you think or feel about something, which may or may not be based on facts.
EXAMPLE: *I think the pizza is too spicy, but that is just my **opinion**.*

oppose (uh POHZ) *verb*   When you **oppose** something, you take a position against it.
EXAMPLE: *Some students **oppose** a dress code, but others want one.*

persuade (puhr SWAYD) *verb*   To **persuade** is to convince someone to think or act a certain way.
EXAMPLE: *I will **persuade** my father to let me go to the party.*

Is truth the same for everyone?

A girl kicks the winning field goal for her school football team. Another girl pins her opponent in a wrestling match. Events like these might surprise you, but there is a good chance they are happening in your town right now. As you read the article, ask yourself: **Should girls be allowed to play on boys' sports teams?**

Leveling the Playing Field

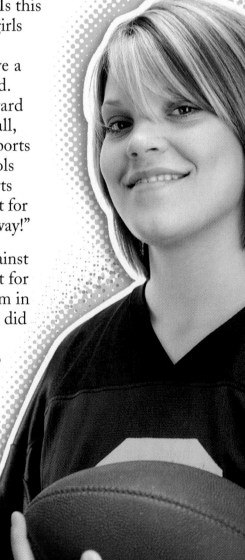

"**O**bviously, boys are better at just about everything. It's just natural," says a student on a sports blog. Is this **opinion** correct? Are boys better at sports than girls are? Should only boys play certain sports?

Until thirty-five years ago, girls did not have a chance to play all of the sports that boys played. Most high schools and colleges had a **bias** toward traditionally male sports like football, basketball, baseball, and wrestling. There were fewer girls' sports offered at most schools. In addition, most schools were quick to **oppose** girls and boys playing sports together. If a girl wanted to play football or try out for the wrestling team, usually the answer was "No way!"

BIG CHANGES After Title IX was passed, it was against the law for a school to keep a girl from trying out for a boys' team—if there was not already a girls' team in the same sport. This made a big difference. Girls did not automatically get to play on boys' teams, but they had the opportunity to try out. Title IX also ordered schools to pay more attention to female athletes and their sports. At the time, Title IX was described as creating a "level playing field" for school athletes, regardless of gender.

Today, girls are allowed to play on boys' ▶ school football teams. It has not always been that way.

The supporters of Title IX did not **persuade** everyone, however. Strong arguments were raised in **opposition**. Almost four decades after Title IX was passed into law, the debate goes on.

HOW WELL CAN SHE PLAY? People who are against Title IX will **inform** you of their concerns. One **opinion** is that the quality of boys' teams suffers when girls are included. Some think that a basketball team with ten boys and a girl will not be competitive against a team of eleven boys.

Supporters of Title IX, however, point out that female athletes still have to try out for the team. The girls have to be talented enough to make the team in the first place. If a girl makes the team, she is skilled enough to play on it.

One teammate of a female basketball player in a boys' league does not think the quality of his team has declined. "We don't mind that she's a girl," he says. "She scores a lot of points; she can dribble, and she doesn't let them get inside."

In 2003, Annika Sorenstam played in a professional golf tournament usually restricted to men.

WILL SHE GET HURT? Some opponents of Title IX are **persuaded** that boys and girls should not play on the same team because of physical differences. Even if a boy and girl are exactly the same age, height, and weight, after age eleven or twelve, the boy will tend to have more muscle. Some girls might get injured trying to play against stronger boys. Some male athletes share this fear. They are afraid they might accidentally hurt female competitors. These boys feel they have to hold back in competition against girls. This concern about injuries can decrease the quality of the game, people say.

Title IX supporters, on the other hand, think this argument is **misinformed.** They point out that everybody grows at a different rate. If you compare all the 13-year-olds in a school, you will probably find some girls who are physically stronger than the average boy. Some boys might be weaker than the average girl. Some stronger girls might play better on a boys' team than some weaker boys.

CAN SHE KEEP UP? Finally, some suggest that girls who play on boys' teams will burn out more quickly than girls who compete on girls' teams. As adults, they may not continue playing at the same level. These people suggest that it is better for female athletes to use their talents on girls' teams so they will stay competitive.

Supporters of Title IX do not find these points **persuasive**. They admit that adult women rarely get to compete against men in sports, but they say a lot of women are talented enough to do so. Golfer Annika Sorenstam, for example, has competed in a men's Professional Golf Association (PGA) tournament.

How will Title IX shape school sports in the future? Only one thing seems certain. **Opinionated** people will continue to take to the playing field to debate the issue.

WRAP IT UP

Find It on the Page

1. List three arguments people have against girls playing boys' sports.

2. List three reasons given in the article why girls should be able to play boys' sports.

3. Which female athlete competed with male golfers in a PGA tournament?

Use Clues

4. Why do you think the debate about Title IX is still going on after thirty–five years?

5. How do you think Title IX has changed how schools plan sports programs for students?

6. What would you suggest a girl do if she wants to play football? Give reasons for your answer.

Connect to the Big Question

After reading this article, do you agree that boys and girls should have the same sports opportunities in school? Explain your answer.

Real-Life Connection

What should happen to children and teens who commit serious crimes? Copy the chart below to note the arguments on each side.

Position	Arguments For	Arguments Against
Keep young offenders in the juvenile system.		
Treat all offenders alike, no matter what their age.		

WORD BANK

contradict (kahn truh DIKT) *verb*   When you **contradict** someone, you argue against what he or she says.
EXAMPLE: *I thought the movie was great, but I know my sister will **contradict** me and say it was bad.*

doubtful (DOWT fuhl) *adjective*   Something is **doubtful** when you are uncertain that it is true.
EXAMPLE: *Natalia is **doubtful** that the team will be able to get to the finals.*

observation (ahb suhr VAY shuhn) *noun*   An **observation** is something you witness or a comment you make about what you have seen.
EXAMPLE: *The planetarium is open tonight for **observation** of the meteor shower.*

represent (re pri ZENT) *verb*   To **represent** is to stand for someone or something.
EXAMPLE: *Mei Lee will go to the state capital to **represent** our school at the debate match.*

theory (THEE uh ree) *noun*   A **theory** is a central idea on which you base an argument.
EXAMPLE: *It is Shanti's **theory** that studying for an extra hour will improve her test scores.*

Is truth the same for everyone?

On the news, you see a judge sentence someone to years in prison. The camera cuts to the convicted person. His head is down. His shoulders shake with sobs. Then he looks up. You see that he is a boy your age. As you read the article, ask yourself: Should kids be treated differently from adults when they commit crimes?

SEPARATE JUSTICE

What happens when a kid commits a crime? Did you know there are two separate justice systems, one for kids and the other for adults? Adult offenders are tried in criminal court. They serve their sentences in prison. Children and young teens, however, are usually handled by the juvenile justice system.

The juvenile system is based on the **theory** of rehabilitation, or helping people change their behavior. For this reason, young offenders are sent to special juvenile detention facilities, not adult prisons. They serve their sentences under close **observation.** They have access to help from counselors and teachers. They learn to live crime-free. If they do well in the system, young offenders are released by the age of 21. Juvenile court records are kept sealed, so offenders have no criminal history.

In reality, the choice of what to do with young criminals depends on a number of factors. How old is the offender? How serious or violent was the crime? Where was the crime committed? Every state has a different policy.

When kids commit serious crimes, society faces a difficult choice.

▼

CHANGING PATTERNS The choice used to be more clear-cut. In the past, offenders under the age of 16 were almost always handled by the juvenile court system. In the late 1980s, however, things began to change. School shootings like the one at Colorado's Columbine High School in 1999 grabbed media headlines. Crimes by teens seemed to be on the rise. People became **doubtful** about the juvenile justice system.

Many states changed their laws. It became easier for people under 16 to be tried and punished as adults. In some states, kids as young as 10 could find themselves in the adult criminal system—not only on murder charges, but also for charges of drug use or property crimes, like car theft.

> Since 1985, the number of kids tried as adults has not stayed constant.

Since 1985, the number of kids tried as adults has not stayed constant. These changes reflect the ongoing argument about separate justice for juveniles and adults. Depending on which side is supported by public opinion, the number of young people tried as adults goes up or down.

JUSTICE FOR JUVENILES Many people support a separate justice system for young people. They say that kids can turn their lives around if they get help. Put teens in the adult system, they argue, and you take away that chance. Prison can become a school for learning violence and crime where the only teachers are adult inmates. "If you really want to create a monster," one expert warns, "see what happens to a child who is locked up in prison for years."

Those who support a juvenile justice system **observe** that sending kids to adult prisons does not scare them out of lives of crime. The opposite is true, they say. Research shows that young offenders who spend time in prison are more likely than other juvenile criminals to commit other crimes in the future and be sent back to prison.

JUSTICE FOR ADULTS On the other side of the debate are many people who **doubt** the benefits of separate justice systems based on age. They **contradict** the argument that kids deserve special treatment from the law. Those who disagree with the juvenile justice system argue that kids who commit adult crimes should pay adult consequences. Society should not have to pay to rehabilitate a juvenile offender, they argue. Juvenile detention programs and the services they offer **represent** a much higher cost to citizens than adult prisons do.

Another strong argument comes from crime victims. Many fear that violent kids cannot be rehabilitated. They worry about releasing violent young offenders at the age of 21. A relative of a victim put it this way: "When it's a vicious, brutal crime, I don't want those guys living next to anybody's family again." Criminals should be punished, regardless of their age.

JUSTICE FOR ALL These **contradictory** arguments have the same goal at heart: justice for everyone concerned. However, balancing justice for young offenders with justice for the victims of their crimes is not an easy task. The question remains, what is the best way to make the punishment fit the crime?

WRAP IT UP

Find It on the Page

1. What are three things that go into the decision to send a young person to juvenile or criminal court?

2. List two ways in which the juvenile justice system and the adult criminal system differ.

3. What type of events caused states to begin making it easier to try kids as adults?

Use Clues

4. Why might juvenile detention centers cost more to operate than adult prisons?

5. Why do you think kids who spend time in prison are more likely to commit other crimes than kids who go through the juvenile system?

6. Should every state have the same policy about treating young offenders? Why or why not?

Connect to the Big Question

After reading the article, do you think having separate systems of justice based on age is a good idea? Explain your answer.

Real-Life Connection

Read each statement. On your own paper, write whether you agree or disagree.

1. New development is always better for a community than saving old neighborhoods.

2. The government has the right to take private property.

3. The needs of the whole community are more important than what a few people want.

Check It Out

In the United States, land is either public or private.

- Private land is owned by individuals, companies, or groups. Homes and shopping malls are built on private land.

- Public land is owned by everyone, but it is managed by the government. Public land is often used for highways, parks, and schools.

arrange (uh RAYNJ) *verb*   When you **arrange** something, you put it in order or prepare for it.
EXAMPLE: *Minh told Sam to **arrange** the chairs in a circle.*

evidence (E vuh duhns) *noun*   **Evidence** is proof that something is true or knowledge you use to back up an argument.
EXAMPLE: *The muddy paw prints are **evidence** that the dog was here.*

fantasy (FAN tuh see) *noun*   A **fantasy** is something that is unreal or imagined.
EXAMPLE: *I am reading a **fantasy** book about talking dragons.*

investigate (in VES tuh gayt) *verb*   To **investigate** something is to look at it carefully to find out the truth.
EXAMPLE: *For her report, Caitlin will **investigate** local sources of air pollution.*

prove (proov) *verb*   When you **prove** something, you show that it is true or correct.
EXAMPLE: *Cal showed us the TV clip to **prove** that he was on the news.*

THE BIG ?

Is truth the same for everyone?

You are excited to hear about plans to build a new sports stadium in your neighborhood. There is just one catch: Your home, and your neighbors' homes, will have to be knocked down to make room for the construction. As you read the article, ask yourself: Who should decide how land is used?

This Land Is *Whose* Land?

You wake up in the middle of the night to the sound of soldiers banging on your door. They are here to take your family's land for the government. You do not have a choice. You have to **arrange** for somewhere else to live, right now. No one pays your family for everything you have lost.

This sounds like a nightmare. For centuries, however, this scary **fantasy** was a reality in Europe. Kings could take what they wanted without answering to anyone. That is why Thomas Jefferson added a special phrase to the Bill of Rights. The Fifth Amendment to the Constitution says, "Private property [shall not] be taken for public use, without just compensation."

EMINENT DOMAIN The Fifth Amendment does not completely limit the government's power. Under a process called "eminent domain," governments can take private property if they can **prove** that it is for "public use." The government must offer the landowner a just price for the property.

Eminent domain can be a good tool for improving communities. When cities need land for bridges and schools, they may **investigate** buying the land from private owners. If the owners refuse, the city can force them to turn over the land.

▲ Governments often use eminent domain to improve neighborhoods.

Cities can also use eminent domain to clean up neighborhoods with **evidence** of blight, such as abandoned buildings.

How do governments define "public use"? It is usually something that all the people in the community can benefit from. Parks and highways are good examples. Sometimes, though, "public use" can be less concrete. What about a new sports stadium, or a shopping mall, or a privately owned hotel?

A SUPREME COURT CASE In 2000, a private developer wanted to build a new hotel complex in New London, Connecticut. About 70 people owned homes and buildings on the ocean-front site the developer hoped to use. Most of the people accepted the company's offer to buy their land. Seven owners refused to sell.

▲

Public protests like this one express people's concerns about the unfair use of eminent domain.

The developer asked the city government to use eminent domain to take the land from the holdouts. The city agreed. It claimed that the **arrangement** would be good for the city's economy. The hotel would bring in tourist money, so it qualified as "public use."

The homeowners sued the city. They did not want to sell their homes to make room for a hotel. One owner's home had been in the family for over 100 years. The owners protested that the hotel did not meet the standard of public use. "They are simply taking our property from us private owners and giving it to another private owner to develop," said one homeowner.

The case was appealed to the Supreme Court. In 2005, the Court ruled in favor of New London. It said that cities could use eminent domain to seize private property for just about any reason.

NEW QUESTIONS The Supreme Court's decision was extremely unpopular. A recent survey found that more than 98 percent of those surveyed disagreed with the decision.

Many people claim that the New London case was not isolated. They say governments have been using eminent domain against people in poor, urban neighborhoods for years. According to **investigators** from the Institute for Justice, thousands of poor people have been forced to leave their homes in order to make room for baseball stadiums, condominiums, and even parking lots. Governments declare whole neighborhoods to be blighted in order to force people out. Some refer to this as eminent domain abuse. They say its benefits are **unproven.**

Since the New London case, some states have passed stricter eminent domain laws in order to protect citizens. In communities like Brooklyn's Melrose Commons neighborhood, the government and residents are working more closely together. Some cities have promised that people can stay in their homes if they want to. They will buy land for new development only from people who want to sell. This is a much slower way to change a neighborhood, but it helps insure that the rights of individuals and communities are protected.

WRAP IT UP

Find It on the Page

1. What part of the Constitution protects the rights of private property owners?

2. In the New London eminent domain case, which side did the Supreme Court favor?

3. How did the city of New London justify using eminent domain for a hotel?

Use Clues

4. Why do you think the Supreme Court's decision was so unpopular with Americans?

5. What can governments learn from the experience of the Melrose Commons community?

6. When the rights of private owners and the needs of the community are in conflict, what should come first? Explain your answer.

Connect to the Big Question

After reading the article, who do you think should decide what defines "public use" when it comes to land and development? Explain your answer.

Real-Life Connection

Study the chart below. Based on the title and headings, what do you think this article will focus on? Copy the chart and use it to jot down your ideas.

Heading	Prediction
Title: Laws That Work for Kids Who Work	
Subhead 1: A Tangle of Laws	
Subhead 2: Work and Safety	
Subhead 3: Work and School	
Subhead 4: Working for Better Laws	

WORD BANK

doubtful (DOWT fuhl) *adjective*   Something is **doubtful** when you are uncertain that it is true.
EXAMPLE: *With this rain coming down, it is **doubtful** that the baseball game will start on time.*

factual (FAK chuh wuhl) *adjective*   Something that is **factual** is true or real.
EXAMPLE: *That movie was based on a **factual** account of a World War II battle.*

illogical (il LAHJ i kuhl) *adjective*   Something that goes against what is reasonable or expected is **illogical.**
EXAMPLE: *On the TV show* Star Trek, *Mr. Spock always accused Captain Kirk of being **illogical.***

objective (uhb JEK tiv) *adjective*   When you are **objective,** you try to separate your feelings about something from the facts.
EXAMPLE: *Even though she disagreed, Sasha tried to be **objective** about her friend's arguments.*

variation (ver ee AY shuhn) *noun*   A **variation** is a change or difference from the usual pattern.
EXAMPLE: *The marching band presented a **variation** of their usual halftime show.*

Is truth the same for everyone?

You want to get a job. Surprise! It is harder than you think. Employers say they are not allowed to hire someone as young as you are. There are laws limiting the kind of work you can do and the number of hours you can do it. As you read the article, ask yourself: **Do young workers need the protection of special laws?**

Laws That Work for Kids Who Work

Every summer, more than 4 million American teens look for jobs. What is the biggest obstacle they face? It is **doubtful** your first guess would be the government. Yet laws can actually make it tough for young adults to get jobs.

Teen labor laws were not intended to keep kids from working. They were designed to protect young workers on the job. Many people believe that the laws have become confusing and outdated, however. They may be causing young workers more harm than good. Many say it is time for a change.

A TANGLE OF LAWS One problem with teen labor laws is that they are not standardized. There are different laws for different age groups, different occupations, and different tasks. For example, kids under the age of fourteen are not supposed to work for money at all—unless they work on farms. Kids as young as ten can get jobs in agriculture. That law made sense when most Americans lived in rural areas, but it is outdated now.

▲ Labor laws limit the kinds of jobs teens can have.

Depending on the state, kids under the ages of 14 and 16 are not supposed to work in dangerous jobs. There are lots of **illogical** exceptions, however. Young teens cannot work as roofers, because they might fall. Yet they can do many other jobs that require climbing tall ladders, like trimming trees and painting bridges. Once kids reach the age of sixteen, many of those laws suddenly change. Teens over sixteen can work almost anywhere.

All this **variation** makes it hard for both employers and kids to keep track of what is legal. Employers who break labor laws must pay costly fines. Rather than take that risk, many employers simply will not hire young people. It can be hard for young teens to find jobs as anything other than fast-food workers and retail sales clerks.

> A labor researcher says, "We haven't been paying enough attention to the dangers."

WORK AND SAFETY You might argue that it would be easier to get rid of the laws altogether. An **objective** look, however, may convince you that there are good reasons for teen labor laws. One of those reasons is safety. Work is dangerous for kids, even when the job itself is not hazardous. Each year, more than 230,000 kids under eighteen are injured on the job. That is an average of one injury every two minutes. Many of these injuries are serious. Some are fatal.

Laws alone cannot prevent all these injuries. **Undoubtedly,** some kids ignore safety measures and do risky things. Employers do not always enforce the rules or give kids the training they need to work safely. Having laws in place, however, is at least a start toward protecting teens on the job.

Some argue teens need more laws enforcing safety on the job, not fewer. "Most teenagers work. Their work can be dangerous, and we haven't been paying enough attention to the dangers. We can do better," says one researcher.

WORK AND SCHOOL Some laws are designed to protect young people's real job: getting an education. Laws limit the number of hours teens can work, especially during the school year. It is hard to juggle class time, a job, and homework. Working too much may cost kids more than a good night's sleep. Studies show that when teens work more than 20 hours in a school week, they are more likely to get poor grades, use alcohol and drugs, and drop out of school.

On the other hand, there is **factual** evidence that a little work can be a good thing. Teens who limit job time to fewer than 15 hours a week actually get *better* grades and are more organized than those who do not work at all.

Every teen is different, of course. That is why some argue that it should be parents, not the government, who decide what work schedule is best. People who make this argument say that individuals can look at the information that is specific to their lives and make informed decisions. The government can only make generalized decisions.

WORKING FOR BETTER LAWS Teens will continue to work. It is important to sort out the tangle of **varying** teen labor laws. Many people are seeking ways to keep kids safe while not limiting their job possibilities. That is a goal worth working for.

WRAP IT UP

Find It on the Page

1. What is the one occupation in which kids as young as ten can legally work?

2. Give one example of how teen labor laws can be illogical.

3. Give one reason why laws alone cannot prevent all teen job injuries.

Use Clues

4. Should there be fewer safety laws or more safety laws for young teens? Explain your answer.

5. What could explain the connection between working more than twenty hours a week and being more likely to use alcohol or drugs?

6. What changes in teen labor laws might make employers more willing to hire young people?

Connect to the Big Question

After reading the article, would you agree that young workers need stronger laws to protect them than those that apply to adults? Why or why not?

Real-Life Connection

How do ratings affect the movies and TV shows you see, the music you buy, and the video games you play? Copy the word web below, and jot down your thoughts about ratings.

Ratings

WORD BANK

control (kuhn TROHL) *verb*   When you **control** something, you guide it or rule over it.
EXAMPLE: *My sister and I fight over who gets to **control** the radio on long car trips.*

illogical (il LAHJ i kuhl) *adjective*   Something that goes against what is reasonable or expected is **illogical.**
EXAMPLE: *Sierra admits her daydream of being the next big singing star is **illogical,** because she really cannot sing a note.*

observation (ahb suhr VAY shuhn) *noun*   An **observation** is something you witness or a comment you make about what you have seen.
EXAMPLE: *Based on his **observation** of the weather, the coach cancelled practice.*

opinion (uh PIN yuhn) *verb*   An **opinion** is the way you think or feel about something, which may or may not be based on facts.
EXAMPLE: *Not everyone in my family shares my **opinion** about the loud music I play.*

theory (THEE uh ree) *noun*   A **theory** is a central idea on which you base an argument.
EXAMPLE: *The detective had a **theory** about why the suspect committed the crime.*

Is truth the same for everyone?

A mom and a young teen argue in the video game store. "You are not buying that game," the mom insists. "It is rated M. It's too violent." The teen answers, "I saved my own money for this game. All my friends have it. Who cares about ratings?" As you read the article, ask yourself: What purpose do rating systems serve?

Debating the Ratings

M for Mature. PG-13. TV-14. R-rated. "Viewer discretion advised." "Explicit content." Everywhere you turn, there are ratings and warning labels. You cannot pick up a CD or settle into a movie theater seat without being reminded that people are worried about what you see and hear.

Who are those people, anyway? Who gave them the power to control your entertainment choices? More importantly, what do they think they are protecting you from—and do you really need protection?

WHO RATES? In the United States, ratings are voluntary. That means that the makers and sellers of products like CDs and movies set the ratings. Ratings do not have the power of government laws. They represent the raters' **opinions** alone.

Movie ratings, the oldest rating system, are assigned by a group of volunteers who watch movies before they are released. These volunteers are all parents of kids aged five to seventeen, not film experts or psychologists. Their names are never made public.

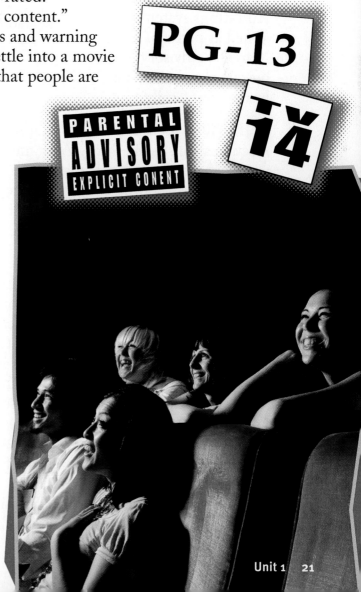

Based on **observations,** the volunteers decide whether a movie has more adult content than kids should see. If so, they rate the movie R, which means "restricted." Parents should not bring or allow children to see the movie.

Wait a minute—parents? What are *they* doing here? All ratings systems are aimed at parents. The "Parental Advisory" sticker on a CD and the letters on a video game box are supposed to guide those who *really* **control** what you see and hear—your family.

MAJOR RATING SYSTEMS			
Medium	Year Began	Number of Possible Ratings	Warning Ratings
Movies	1968	5	PG-13, R, NC-17
Music	1990	1	Parental Advisory
Television	1990s	7	TV-14, MA
Video Games	1994	5	T, M, AO

Information is from "The Ratings Game: Choosing Your Child's Entertainment" from the American Academy of Pediatrics.

WHERE DID RATINGS COME FROM? Rating systems usually develop as a reaction against something. With music, for example, the reaction was against sexually explicit language and violent lyrics. In 1985, Tipper Gore, the wife of former Vice-President Al Gore, was shocked when she listened to a CD she bought for her daughter. Mrs. Gore helped convince the music industry to add Parental Advisory stickers to CDs.

DO RATINGS WORK? You are probably the best person to answer that question. Most kids can find ways around the ratings if they want to. Many theatres do not ask for identification when kids buy tickets for R-rated movies. Kids can watch R-rated movies on DVD or cable (if they can get around the locks parents install). A survey of video store owners **observed** that 78 percent of all M-rated games are bought by kids under sixteen, with no adult present. That is something ratings are supposed to prevent.

Ratings are tough to enforce. In addition, they may actually encourage what they try to prevent. There is something called the "forbidden fruit" **theory,** which says people are drawn to things they are not supposed to have. According to this **theory,** ratings and warning labels become sales pitches. CBS news commentator Andy

Rooney joked about the TV shows that carry the caution, "viewer discretion advised." "The suggestion is that children shouldn't watch it," Rooney said. "What it does, of course, is alert kids to watch."

PROBLEMS WITH RATINGS Kids are not the only ones who have trouble with ratings. Both parents and producers think movie ratings are confusing and **illogical.** People complain that music warning stickers are biased because they are required only on rock, rap, and hip hop CDs. Finally, many adults believe that decisions about entertainment content should be kept strictly in the family.

Other people think ratings do not go far enough. Every year, government officials try to pass laws to limit what kids can see and hear. In 2003, for example, a California legislator proposed a national ban on sales of violent video games to anyone under eighteen. The law failed, but new ones like it are introduced all the time.

Laws controlling content introduce new concerns. They are a form of censorship. **Theoretically,** that conflicts with the First Amendment right to free speech. Voluntary ratings have many flaws, and they are very controversial. Compared to laws, however, they may be the better choice.

WRAP IT UP

Find It on the Page

1. Who pushed the music industry to start using warning stickers?

2. Give an example of how kids can get around ratings.

3. What often causes rating systems to develop?

Use Clues

4. Do you agree with the "forbidden fruit" theory explained in the article? Why?

5. Which of the major rating systems do you think is least helpful in guiding parents to make choices? Why?

6. In your opinion, should the Internet have a rating system? Explain.

Connect to the Big Question

After reading this article, has your attitude toward ratings changed? Explain your answer.

Real-Life Connection

The sentences below are about forensic science. On a separate sheet of paper, write whether you agree or disagree with each statement.

1. TV crime dramas show how crime is solved in the real world.
2. Fingerprinting is a sure way to show that someone is guilty of a crime.
3. DNA evidence has helped free many innocent people from prison.

Check It Out

Forensics experts analyze evidence, such as fingerprints, hair, blood, and DNA.

- We all have DNA in our bodies. We get our DNA from our parents.
- DNA determines eye color, height, and other physical characteristics.
- Your DNA profile, or sequence of DNA materials, is unique to you.

WORD BANK

analyze (A nuh lyz) *verb*   When you **analyze** something, you study its parts and see how they fit together.
EXAMPLE: *The teacher had to **analyze** how Danny did the math problem to figure out why he got the wrong answer.*

confirm (kuhn FUHRM) *verb*   To **confirm** something is to agree with it or demonstrate that it is true.
EXAMPLE: *Yolanda asked her teacher to **confirm** the date of the test.*

evidence (E vuh duhns) *noun*   **Evidence** is proof that something is true, or it is knowledge you use to back up an argument.
EXAMPLE: *The hairs my dog left behind were **evidence** he had broken the rules and sat on the couch.*

investigate (in VES tuh gayt) *verb*   To **investigate** something is to look at it carefully to find out the truth.
EXAMPLE: *For her science project, Mashika decided to **investigate** what was making the water in a nearby lake so dirty.*

prove (proov) *verb*   When you **prove** something, you show that it is true or correct.
EXAMPLE: *Eddie asked his mother to sign his report card so that he could **prove** to his teachers that she had read it.*

Is truth the same for everyone?

In a courtroom, people usually have different ideas about the truth. Jurors have to decide who they believe is telling the truth. Forensic science helps jurors make this decision. As you read the article, ask yourself: How much trust should jurors put in forensics?

The CSI Effect

Americans love TV dramas about crime scene **investigation** (CSI). On these shows, crimes are always quickly and correctly solved. TV detectives **investigate** a crime scene and find fingerprints, hairs, DNA, or other **evidence.** The evidence is in good shape. Scientists run tests on the **evidence,** and the results **prove** who committed the crime.

Real forensic science seldom works so smoothly. Most crime scenes do not include fingerprints or DNA **evidence.** If there is **evidence,** it may be in bad shape. Fingerprints may be smeared. DNA **evidence** may be contaminated. Even when evidence is usable, it takes time to test and **analyze** it. Results come in after weeks, not hours, of waiting, and they still might not be accurate.

THE WRONG MAN Still, many people assume that real forensic science is like the forensics on TV. When these people serve on a jury, they mistakenly believe that forensic science is always right. This common problem, called the CSI effect, has sent innocent people to prison. Take, for instance, Riky Jackson. He was convicted of murder and wrongly imprisoned for more than two years.

▲ **A forensic scientist preserves evidence at a crime scene.**

At his trial, three fingerprint **analysts** said Jackson's fingerprints matched prints at the murder scene. The **analysts** convinced jurors that Jackson was the murderer, and they quickly found him guilty. Jackson's lawyer was shocked. He believed Jackson was innocent, but he needed more proof. The lawyer arranged to have the fingerprint **analysis** sent to the FBI. Experts there were able to confirm that Jackson was innocent. The fingerprints did not match. A judge believed the FBI and set Jackson free. Still, an important question remains: How did three different fingerprint **analysts** make the same mistake?

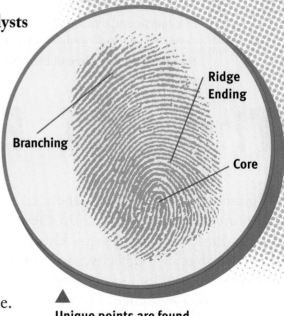

Unique points are found in each fingerprint. Those points are what the computer uses to search for a match.

FEW STANDARDS One possible explanation is that the **analysts** were badly trained. A fingerprint **analyst** does not need a special license. Most **analysts** learn on the job, and the methods they learn may be incorrect.

Another possible explanation for the mistake is that the **analysis** was done too fast. Police are often under pressure to solve a crime quickly. They, in turn, might pressure fingerprint **analysts** to rush. Detectives may also accidentally influence fingerprint **analysts.** If detectives believe that someone is guilty of a crime, they may, without realizing it, make **analysts** think so, too.

Yet another concern is that all **analysts** do not follow the same guidelines. One fingerprint expert explains that "it's up to the examiner to decide how much matching consistency they need between the known and unknown print." Some **analysts** say eight similarities between sets of prints equal a match. Other **analysts** say ten similarities are needed for a match. Others say twelve.

OTHER ERRORS Fingerprint **analysts** are not the only forensics experts who have made mistakes. Errors have been made in every other kind of forensic science as well. One well-known error involved the

Montana state crime lab. The analyst who ran the lab did a hair **analysis** that put an innocent man in prison for fifteen years. In court, the lab **analyst** said that hairs found at a crime scene matched Jimmy Ray Bromgard's hair. He told the court that there was a less than one in 10,000 chance that the hair was not Bromgard's. That statistic was not fact, yet jurors believed the fingerprint **analyst's** statement and found Bromgard guilty.

Bromgard's lawyer asked many times for a new trial. The court always refused. Finally, the lawyer called the Innocence Project. This group of lawyers and law students **investigates** mistakes in criminal trials. Luckily for Bromgard, the Innocence Project agreed to help. The group convinced a judge to order a DNA test, and the test was able to prove that Bromgard was innocent. Finally, he was set free.

DNA **evidence** has, in fact, helped free more than two hundred innocent people wrongly sent to prison. Like other types of forensic science, DNA **analysis** can be helpful. It is almost always right, but, like other types of forensic science, DNA **analysis** is not perfect. It is only as good as the people who use it, and people make mistakes.

WRAP IT UP

Find It on the Page

1. What is the CSI effect?
2. List four ways that real forensic science is different from the forensic science on TV crime dramas.
3. Briefly summarize two court cases in which forensic experts were wrong.

Use Clues

4. Why do you think TV crime dramas do not show forensic science as it really is?

5. Why might the CSI effect make it harder for lawyers to prove that someone is innocent?
6. What changes would you make to help cut back on mistakes in fingerprint analysis?

Connect to the Big Question

After reading the article, how much trust do you think jurors should put in forensic science and why?

Real-Life Connection

Have you ever made a snap decision based on a first impression? Make a copy of the organizer below. Use it to jot down what you learn about first impressions as you read the article.

First Impressions

| How They Work | Where They Came From | Reasons to Trust Them | Reasons for Caution |

WORD BANK

bias (BY uhs) *noun*   To have a **bias** means to prefer or reject one group or one thing over another every time.
EXAMPLE: *Eli did not let his **bias** in favor of the Cougars keep him from appreciating the Redbirds' defense.*

confirm (kuhn FUHRM) *verb*   To **confirm** something is to agree with it or demonstrate that it is true.
EXAMPLE: *Diego clicked the button to **confirm** payment for downloading the music.*

factual (FAK chuh wuhl) *adjective*   Something that is **factual** is true or real.
EXAMPLE: *The newspaper story was not completely **factual**.*

objective (uhb JEK tiv) *adjective*   When you are **objective,** you try to separate your feelings about something from the facts.
EXAMPLE: *I am finding it hard to be **objective** about the grade I got on the final.*

process (PRAH ses) *noun*   A **process** is a set of steps you follow to complete an action.
EXAMPLE: *Pedro's grandmother taught him the **process** for making tamales.*

Is truth the same for everyone?

You meet two kids for the first time. One is wearing a T-shirt with the name of your favorite band. You think, "This kid is cool." The other has on a brown jacket, just like the one the class bully wears. You think, "This kid is scary." As you read the article, ask yourself: **Are first impressions always right?**

At First Sight

Your eyes meet across a crowded room. Boom! Your heart beats faster. You start making plans for a Friday night date, the big dance, your wedding. . . .

Ah, yes—love at first sight. It is the inspiration for at least half of all the songs ever sung or movies ever rented. Is there anything **factual** about this idea of sudden infatuation, or is it just a myth?

Love at first sight may be a Hollywood cliché, but do not dismiss it. New studies **confirm** that first impressions do count. A quick glance sends a whole library of information to your brain, which you process all at once. It is as though your brain downloads a multi-gigabyte file using the highest-speed Internet connection ever. In a nanosecond, your brain makes a judgment based on the information it receives. This whole **process** happens, literally, "in the blink of an eye." It is not conscious or **objective.** You do not think about it at all. You just "know" that the person across the crowded room is your destiny—or not.

Your brain makes snap judgments about people at first sight.

DISLIKE AT FIRST SIGHT? Love at first sight is not the only way your mind responds to first impressions. You may have had the experience of meeting someone for the first time and deciding instantly that there will never be a next time. People account for this dislike at first sight in different ways. "I just got a bad vibe from him," you might say.

> **The brain's ability to decide in a fraction of a second may have developed as a safety device.**

Scientists say we make snap judgments based on first impressions all the time. People make choices about everything from food to new cars this way. You may look for **confirmation** of your instinct by checking references or comparing prices. In most cases, however, that first lightning-fast judgment has the power to sway your decision.

MAKING CONNECTIONS When you take in a first impression, your brain begins **processing** a lot of data at once. The flood of information comes from your eyes, ears, and even your nose. You even pick up subtle clues, like facial expressions or body language that your conscious mind might not notice. Your brain compares this new information with the stored data of your past experiences. That comparison leads to instantaneous judgment.

The brain's ability to decide in a fraction of a second may have developed as a safety device. Early humans had to learn to read their surroundings quickly and react without thinking in order to stay alive. Survival could depend on making the instant connection between a large, snarling animal and the decision to run for your life!

Your brain still carries that life-or-death instinct. Most people shiver at the sound of a wild animal's howl, for example. They melt when they see a cute, helpless baby. That built-in **bias** is so strong that people even tend to be drawn to adults who have babyish features.

THE WRONG IMPRESSION? You can see how first impressions work—but can you trust them? Scientists say your "gut" feelings are generally telling you the truth. "We're often fooled, of course, but we're more often right," says one psychologist. There are some important cautions, though, when it comes to first impressions.

Your judgment is only as good as your data. Your brain can only make decisions based on comparisons with your experience. If your experiences are limited, then the value of your decisions might be limited as well. Negative experiences can also affect your decisions. You might refuse to try a new food, for example, because it looks like something you once tasted and did not like.

People can fool you if they try. Criminals can be very good at appearing innocent. (There is a reason so many gangsters have been nicknamed "Baby Face.") Be especially wary of online first impressions. The Internet erases many of the clues your brain relies on in a real-world encounter.

*First impressions are not **unbiased**.* Unfortunately, prejudice is a part of people's experience, too. First impressions can be warped by stereotypes and can reinforce racism and hatred.

It is always wise to examine your first impressions **objectively** before acting on them. Look at **facts,** not just feelings. In other words, do not start planning that wedding just yet.

WRAP IT UP

Find It on the Page

1. What does your brain do with the information it gathers from a first impression?

2. According to the article, why should people distrust first impressions made online?

3. How did the ability to make snap judgments help early humans survive?

Use Clues

4. Why do you think the human brain is programmed to respond positively to babies' faces?

5. Give an example of how prejudice can make a first impression wrong.

6. How could you test whether a first impression is correct?

Connect to the Big Question

After reading this article, will you be more or less likely to trust your first impressions? Explain your answer.

Real-Life Connection

You have probably heard people talk about "the American dream." What do you think about it? Copy these questions, and answer yes or no to each.

1. Is the American dream about becoming wealthy?
2. Is the American dream only for immigrants?
3. Do people your age care about the American dream?

Check It Out

One version of the American dream is found in the Declaration of Independence. This country's founders believed that all people had a right to "life, liberty, and the pursuit of happiness." They did not try to define what happiness was, and they did not guarantee that people would get it. They hoped, however, that America would be a place where people could be free to follow their dreams.

WORD BANK

contradict (kahn truh DIKT) *verb*　When you **contradict** someone, you argue against what he or she says.
EXAMPLE: *I had to **contradict** Lucie when she said that the statement was false, because I was sure it was true.*

equal (EE kwuhl) *adjective*　Things that are **equal** are the same or fairly balanced.
EXAMPLE: *Greg believes animals deserve **equal** rights with humans.*

essential (i SEN shuhl) *adjective*　When something is **essential,** it is necessary and important.
EXAMPLE: *Getting enough water is **essential** to staying healthy and fit.*

fantasy (FAN tuh see) *noun*　A **fantasy** is something that is unreal or imagined.
EXAMPLE: *In my **fantasy,** I won the lottery, made a music video, and played in the Super Bowl all in the same day.*

persuade (puhr SWAYD) *verb*　To **persuade** is to convince someone to think or act a certain way.
EXAMPLE: *LaKeisha was able to **persuade** her brother to drive us to the movie.*

Is truth the same for everyone?

While channel-surfing, you come across two speakers debating. "The American dream is still alive! It is about freedom!" one argues. "No, it is about money," the other responds. "Nobody can afford the American dream anymore." As you read the article, ask yourself: **Do all Americans have the same American dream?**

American Dreaming

*P*eople come from around the world in search of it. Presidential candidates promise to make it come true. Artists picture it as a house surrounded by a white picket fence, or a flag waving in the breeze. Social activists question whether it is dead. Advertisers try to **persuade** you it is a car or a pair of jeans or a soft drink. Some people fear it is just a **fantasy.**

If you are still confused, that is understandable. You will not find the American dream spelled out in the Constitution. For an idea that is not very well defined, however, the American dream has a powerful hold on people's imaginations. It has been that way for over 400 years.

A CHANGING DREAM Some of the first Europeans to settle in America came with dreams of freedom. They wanted a way of life that was not limited by old ideas about wealth and power. Their American dream was a land in which people had **equal** rights and opportunities. They wanted this freedom not just for themselves, but for their children, and for all generations to come.

However you define it, people have always ▶ been drawn to the American dream.

As America grew and changed, the American dream also changed. Freedom and equality were still important—especially for the millions of immigrants who made it their dream, too. Gradually, however, many people began to associate the American dream with material success. People thought of this country as a place of **fantastic,** unlimited economic opportunity, where any poor kid could eventually become a millionaire.

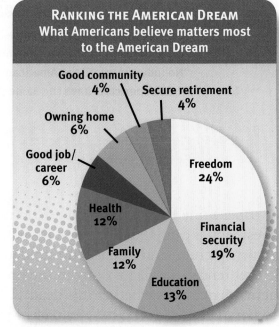

RANKING THE AMERICAN DREAM
What Americans believe matters most to the American Dream

- Good community 4%
- Secure retirement 4%
- Owning home 6%
- Good job/career 6%
- Freedom 24%
- Health 12%
- Financial security 19%
- Family 12%
- Education 13%

Information is from the National League of Cities, 2004.

Often the reality of life in America **contradicts** the American dream. Freedom and economic opportunity are not always available to everyone. In his speeches during the civil rights movement, Martin Luther King, Jr. often demanded a change in the system that provided **unequal** access to the American dream. When Americans cannot achieve the freedom or financial security they long for, they sometimes begin to doubt that the dream is possible. They wonder if they will be able to make a better life for themselves and their families. Other people wonder if the American dream places too much emphasis on material things. Is the American dream really all about wealth, success and fame?

THE DREAM TODAY In recent years, people have taken a new look at the American dream. Polls have asked people to define the dream for themselves and to list the things that are most **essential** for living the dream. Surprisingly, Americans are not as obsessed with wealth and possessions as many people feared. In fact, most adults ranked freedom even higher than financial security. They also ranked education, family, and health much higher than owning a home.

When they used their own words, people described the American dream in countless different ways. Although this may seem to be a **contradiction,** one Web site disagrees. "We are a nation of roughly 301 million people with bloodlines stemming from almost every other nation on the planet," the site notes. "Surely the American dream is not a one-size-fits-all notion." A nation of many cultures is going to have many different dreams.

YOUR AMERICAN DREAM How **persuasive** is the idea of an American dream? How would *you* define it? In a 2005 survey, teens aged thirteen to seventeen overwhelmingly chose "simply being happy" as the best description of the American dream. In comparison to happiness, "being rich or famous" ranked very low on the list. These teens said education, not money, was the most important factor in achieving the dream. Teens in the survey were optimistic, too. When asked if they believed that they would be able to live the American dream as adults, more than 70 percent said yes.

What you believe about the American dream is important because you will determine what shape the dream takes next. In a 2007 graduation speech, Purdue University president Martin C. Jischke told young people that he believed the American dream can be fulfilled. "I believe you are the ones who will do it," he said. "You are our American dream for a better tomorrow."

WRAP IT UP

Find It on the Page

1. In a 2005 survey, what did 70 percent of teens believe about the American dream?

2. What do people often associate the American dream with?

3. What contradiction of the American dream did Martin Luther King, Jr., point out?

Use Clues

4. Would it be wrong to limit the idea of the American dream to economic success? Why?

5. What is the connection between the American dream and immigration?

6. Do you agree that teens' ideas about the American dream are important? Explain your answer.

Connect to the Big Question

After reading this article, would you say that all Americans should define the American dream in the same way? Why or why not?

PROJECT: Write-Around

Answer the Big Question: Is truth the same for everyone?
You have read about issues that center on truth. Now, use what you learned to answer the Unit 1 Big Question (BQ).

STEP 1: Form a Group and Choose
Your first step is to pick Unit 1 articles that you like.
Get together. Find a small group to work with.
Read the list of articles. Discuss which articles listed on the left side of this page were the most interesting to you.
Choose two or more articles. Pick articles that you all agree on.

STEP 2: Reread and Answer the Unit Big Question
Your next step is to answer the Unit BQ in your group.
Reread the articles you chose. As you reread, think about the Unit BQ.
Answer questions. For each article you chose, answer these questions:

- What is the topic, or central issue, of this article?
- According to the article, is there only one "truth" about this topic, or do people disagree?
- How does this article help you understand that there might be different truths, or different ways of thinking about an issue?

Take notes. Write the Unit BQ at the top of a sheet of paper for a write-around. Pass the paper around to group members. Each member has one minute to write an answer to the Unit BQ. Leave room after each response to add notes in step 3.

STEP 3: Discuss and Give Reasons
During this step, discuss your group's Unit BQ answers.
Discuss the answers to the Unit BQ. Explain your answer to the group. Make sure that you use details from the articles to explain your answer. Give each group member a chance to share the reasons for his or her answer.
Write your group's reasons. Add the reasons to your notes.

STEP 4: Summarize the Group's Response

Now, finish the write-around by creating a summary.

Reread your group's answers. Look over your notes and see if your group members agreed. Group members probably agreed that the truth is not the same for everyone, but they may have had different reasons to support their viewpoints.

Summarize the write-around. Be sure that viewpoints are supported with reasons. Choose the reasons that are most convincing. Remember, a summary includes the most important ideas—not all the ideas.

STEP 5: Check and Fix

Next, you and your group will look over your write-around summary to see if it could be improved.

Use the rubric. Use the questions to evaluate your work. Answer each question yes or no. If you would like another opinion about your summary, trade with another group and use the rubric again.

Discuss your evaluations. For your yes answers, think about what you can do to strengthen your summary. If you have any no answers, talk about what you can do to turn each no into a yes.

Improve your summary. After discussing the results of using the rubric, work together to make your summary stronger.

STEP 6: Practice and Present

Get ready to present your write-around and summary to classmates.

Practice what you want to say. You will use your write-around to explain your group's answer to the Unit BQ. You might have each group member present his or her answer. Then a group spokesperson might present the summary.

Present your work. Explain your answer to the Unit 1 BQ to your classmates. In addition, you might post your thoughts about the Unit BQ on a classroom Web page or in a blog.

RUBRIC

Does the summary . . .
- answer the Unit BQ?
- include details from at least two articles in Unit 1?
- show a clear relationship between the answer and the reasons given to support it?
- include the viewpoints of all group members, even if group members disagreed?
- show a clear organization by starting with the answer to the Unit BQ and then supporting that answer with details?

Can all conflicts be resolved?

Two students have different ideas about a poem, but neither student is "right." What other conflicts cannot be resolved? This unit explores conflicts about topics such as computer games, IQ tests, and teen curfew laws. As you read, think about each conflict and the Big Question. Can such conflicts be resolved?

Think about a conflict you were involved in that had no "winner." What was the conflict? Was it resolved? Why or why not?

Real-Life Connection

Most people have seen or played electronic games on computers or with special controls. What comes to mind when you think about these games? Make a word web like the one below. Use it to jot down your ideas.

Electronic Games

WORD BANK

compromise (KAHM pruh myz) *noun*   When you reach a **compromise** with someone else, you both give up something you want in order to settle an argument.
EXAMPLE: *Ray and I both wanted to watch the same television show, so we reached a compromise by taking turns.*

detail (di TAYL) *noun*   A **detail** is a small part of something bigger.
EXAMPLE: *The story had a lot of detail, including descriptions of places and people.*

injury (INJ ree) *noun*   An **injury** is harm or damage done to someone or something.
EXAMPLE: *Tran walked with a limp because of a leg injury.*

interact (in tuhr AKT) *verb*   When you **interact** with people, you exchange information with them.
EXAMPLE: *Ron's shyness makes it difficult for him to interact with his classmates.*

violence (VY luhns) *noun*   **Violence** is the use of physical force to harm someone or to damage property.
EXAMPLE: *Images of violence in movies may give some kids nightmares.*

Can all conflicts be resolved?

Two young people play a computer game in which armies fight a bloody battle. One person says, " Look at the graphics! That game is awesome!" The other says, "No way! The fighting and the blood are not good." What do you think? As you read the article, ask yourself: **Are electronic games simply fun, or can they be harmful?**

Games People Play

▲
Electronic games may cause frustration or anger.

You walk through a dark forest and hear dry leaves crunch under your feet. Your eyes scan every **detail,** every rock and bush, looking for anything suspicious. Suddenly, a fierce-looking warrior swinging a huge sword jumps out from behind a tree. The screaming warrior runs at you. If you cannot stop him, he will cause you serious **injury.**

Quickly, you tap your computer keyboard. Your "life" is saved. Your heart pumps with excitement as you think, "This is a great game!"

TWO VIEWS If you are like most kids, you have probably spent a lot of time playing electronic games. Some games are played on a computer with keyboard strokes. Video games are played on special machines with controls made just for that game. Millions of young people enjoy these games. Parking themselves in front of a screen is a way of life for many teenagers today.

VIOLENCE IN GAMES It is that way of life, the hours spent in front of screens, that worries some psychologists. They worry because many popular games involve characters trying to **injure** each other.

These games are often "first-person" games that put the player in the middle of the **action.** The player takes the role of a character. As that character, the player must **interact** with other characters and objects. The **interactions** may involve **violence.**

Do **violent** games cause **violent** behavior? In a recent study, scientists examined brain scans of teenagers who played video games for thirty minutes. The members of one group played a game that challenged them to race cars. The others played a war-based game in which players used "guns" to "kill" characters.

> Most young people can differentiate between a game and the real world.

Researchers found that the brain activity of kids playing the **violent** game increased in the area that controls emotions. Activity in the areas of self-control and attention decreased. These effects were not seen in kids who played the racing game. The researcher who led the study says, "I think parents should be aware of the relationship between **violent** video game-playing and [the] brain."

One psychologist who studies effects of video games on aggression is concerned about the emotional effects. He points out that unlike violent movies and television shows, which many experts also say cause violent behavior, violent video games allow players to participate in the violence. Players begin to identify with aggressive characters. This active environment is a concern.

GAMES KEEP KIDS INACTIVE Some experts who see games as harmful point out that children and teenagers who spend too much time playing computer games do not get enough exercise. The lack of exercise affects game players' health. Also, playing games for hours takes time away from schoolwork and other activities.

GAMES CAN BE HELPFUL Do the studies mean that all video games are harmful? Not at all, say some people. In games such as the racing game, fast thinking and quick reactions can often make the difference between winning and losing. Playing video games can be good exercise for the brain as well as the hands and eyes. Being in good mental shape comes in handy when studying.

Another belief about video games has to do with the way that they are designed to build players' confidence. Players want challenging games, not games that are dumbed down. Learners who may be frustrated with some types of learning can feel good about their performance in a video game.

Some games also require several players at once. Players learn how to work in a group and how to **compromise** to reach a solution so they can move forward in the game. These are useful skills that some experts see as positive effects of playing computer games.

KNOWING THE DIFFERENCE Experts on both sides of the debate realize that most young people can differentiate between a game and the real world. Most electronic game players know that what they do in a game is not acceptable in real life. However, the debate over whether computer games are harmful or harmless is likely to continue. One parent believes that it is more important to know how much time her kids spend playing a game than which game they are playing. "Let's quit using games as babysitters and do healthful activities," she says.

WRAP IT UP

Find It on the Page

1. How would you define *electronic games*?

2. List two ways in which some computer games can be harmful.

3. List two positive ways computer games may affect players.

Use Clues

4. How might you play a violent computer game and avoid any harmful effects?

5. What do you think could be done to make violent games less violent without losing the excitement of the game?

6. Do you think this article provides enough information for a reader to form an opinion? Explain.

Connect to the Big Question

How did the article affect your opinion about whether electronic games are harmful or harmless?

Real-Life Connection

Think about how you use the Internet. Do you have a profile on a social networking Web site? Respond yes or no to each statement below, and write your thoughts on whether such sites are good places to make friends.

1. I spend more than one hour per day on the Internet.

2. I have a profile page on a social networking site.

3. I have made friends on a social networking site.

Check It Out

About 80 percent of U.S. kids aged twelve to seventeen use the Internet. Almost 50 percent log on each day. Social networking sites are the new places to hang out with current friends and to make new ones.

WORD BANK

consider (kuhn SI duhr) *verb*   When you **consider** something, you think about it carefully.
EXAMPLE: *Meg will **consider** her options before choosing a new pair of running shoes.*

insecurity (in si KYOOR uh tee) *noun*   **Insecurity** refers to a lack of confidence.
EXAMPLE: *Bryan's **insecurity** turned to confidence when his teacher complimented his artwork.*

mislead (mis LEED) *verb*   When you **mislead** people, you give them the wrong idea about something.
EXAMPLE: *Some ads **mislead** people into thinking that they will get rich quickly.*

reveal (ri VEEL) *verb*   When you show something that has been hidden, you **reveal** it.
EXAMPLE: *I opened the door to **reveal** my newly cleaned room.*

viewpoint (VYOO poynt) *noun*   A **viewpoint** is the way a person looks at or thinks about something.
EXAMPLE: *My parent's **viewpoint** about loud music is very different from mine!*

THE BIG ?

Can all conflicts be resolved?

Think of all the ways you use the Internet: playing games, downloading music, or even working on your homework. What do you think about the Internet as a place to hang out with your friends? How about as a place to make new friends? As you read the article, ask yourself: **Can people become true friends if they never meet?**

Cyber Friends

"R U THERE?" Your schoolwork is done for the day. Now it is time to hang out with friends. Instead of picking up the phone or heading out the door, you sit down at your computer. You log on to a special Web site and find your friend's personal Web page. You type in a question: "R U there?" He types back, "Hi! I've been waiting 4 U!" Soon you are talking about the things friends talk about. You can do this because you both belong to a social networking Web site.

SOCIAL NETWORKING WEB SITES Millions of kids keep in touch with friends today on social networking sites, such as MySpace, Friendster, and Xanga. They make new friends at these sites, too. The sites provide personal Web pages, or profiles, for their members. To some teens, a social networking page is like an online room they can decorate to **reveal** information about themselves. Any feelings of **insecurity** they may have in regular face-to-face interactions with people disappear online. Some profile pages tell so much about a person, the profile becomes an extension of the person's life.

Are computers replacing friendships like these? ▼

One teenager with a page on MySpace explained, "Your page is like your personality."

PUBLIC OR PRIVATE Once a personal page is set up, a member can decide who will be able to view the page. Social networking sites allow members to make their pages as public or as private as they like. Most personal pages have a list of "friends." These "friends" are allowed access to the member's page. A friends list may contain names of people the page owner has never met in person. On social networking sites, members get to know other members by looking at their profiles. They contact people they might like to know. Sometimes new friends live in the same town or even go to the same school. More and more people are making friends with others who live far away.

GLOBAL REACH Imagine sharing your deepest thoughts with your friends at home. Now imagine sharing them with strangers in distant countries. That is one way that social networking sites have changed the nature of friendships. By early 2006, MySpace had more than 67 million members from all over the world. A profile page with open access could be read by many people.

To some teenagers, sharing thoughts with people far away is exciting. Their **viewpoint** is that the people reading the profile are potential friends. To them, the possibility of getting to know someone from another country is an adventure. The exchange of ideas between two cultures may even help **lead** to understanding and tolerance. It is difficult to **consider** someone an enemy when you share the same taste in music!

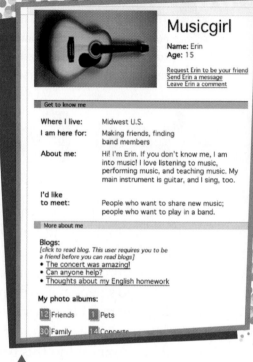

Think about the information before you post it.

STAYING SAFE Social network members need to be careful about their new "friends." Not everyone who browses a personal profile has good intentions. Some people try to **mislead** others. In some cases, this is more a trick than a desire to harm anyone. For example, some teenagers use other people's pictures on their profile pages instead of displaying photos of themselves. The page may contain information that is fanciful rather than truthful. Profiled individuals could lie about their age just to appear older. There are people who create false profiles to fool others. Some people who say they are "friends" have harmful intentions.

Teenagers who enjoy social networking sites need to recognize that information they want to keep private may not stay **secure.** It can be passed around from friend to friend. Before long, information can be well out of the private circle of people you know. Perhaps before you post you should take into **consideration** the same question that you would before you **reveal** something to a friend in real life: Who needs to know this about me?

WRAP IT UP

Find It on the Page

1. How would you define a social networking Web site?

2. List one way in which social networking Web sites help people make friends.

3. Compare and contrast how social networking sites can be a positive way and a negative way to make friends.

Use Clues

4. What suggestions would you have to make social networking sites better and safer?

5. What do you think would happen if social networking sites limited the type of information that could be posted on a person's individual page?

6. What is your opinion about friendships formed through these Web sites? Explain.

Connect to the Big Question

Do you think you can have a close relationship with a person without having any face-to-face contact? Explain why or why not.

Real-Life Connection

This article explains one method people can use to communicate with each other. Read the title of the article and the section titles. What do you think the article will be about? Copy the chart on your own paper and write your predictions.

Section	Prediction
Article Title: Text Talk	
Bridging the Gap	
Little Words, Big Thoughts	
A Way to Guide	
The Downsides	

WORD BANK

irritate (IR uh tayt) *verb*   When you **irritate** someone, you annoy or anger the person.
EXAMPLE: *Ava knew that her constant teasing would **irritate** her brother.*

respond (ri SPAHND) *verb*   When you **respond** to something, you react or answer back.
EXAMPLE: *Anna wanted to **respond** to the joke but could not think of anything to say.*

solution (suh LOO shuhn) *noun*   A **solution** is an answer to a problem.
EXAMPLE: *Luis's **solution** to the math problem involved multiplying and changing fractions into decimals.*

substitute (SUHB stuh toot) *noun*   A **substitute** is something or someone that takes the place of another.
EXAMPLE: *Fruit juice can be a healthful **substitute** for soda.*

victorious (vik TOHR ee uhs) *adjective*   A **victorious** person has won something, such as a contest or a race.
EXAMPLE: *The **victorious** runner waved her arms in celebration.*

Can all conflicts be resolved?

A message pops up on your cell phone. To an adult, it might look like a mishmash of letters and numbers. To you, though, it has a clear meaning. Text messaging is a language unto itself that some adults do not understand. As you read the article, ask yourself: **Can text messaging be a way to help kids and adults communicate?**

text talk

BRIDGING THE GAP THNX 4 YA help W/ project! CU 2moro. SOTMG. Translation: Thanks for your help with the project! See you tomorrow. I'm short on time and must go.

Look out, kids! You are not the only ones texting. Adults are catching on to the trend. They are getting good at it, too. A recent study shows that, in one year, the number of text-messaging adults aged forty-five to sixty-four grew about seven times faster than the number of texting teens under age eighteen! The speedy communication tool is very useful when co-workers need to "talk" during meetings. Adults are getting into the habit of texting their friends and family. In fact, staying in touch with their kids is one of the most important reasons adults give for texting. This unique language may be one **solution** to bridging the generation gap.

Nothing seems to **irritate** teenagers more than what they see as prying from parents. To the parents, though, their prying is really a way to understand and stay in touch with their kids. Texting may be one way to **solve** communication issues for kids and parents.

CU 2MORO

Adults are the fastest-growing group of text message users. ▶

LITTLE WORDS, BIG THOUGHTS Kids like using text messaging because it is quick and fun. Messages sent from parent to child feel less like parents prying than simple interest in their children's lives. Because the messages are short, kids may not feel they are being nagged. **Irritations** are avoided all the way around. Kids actually feel somewhat **victorious** in winning their parents over to a language the kids feel they created.

COMMON TEXTING ABBREVIATIONS	
4	For
CU	See you
GR8	Great!
IMHO	In my humble opinion
B4	Before
2MORO	Tomorrow
J/C	Just checking
SOTMG	Short on time; must go
THNX	Thanks
W/	With

Parents also like that text messaging is quick. More importantly, though, their kids actually **respond.** Starting a conversation about how school is going seems to be a lot easier using text messages. One parent said about texting her teenage daughter, "You know, if I had asked her at dinner, 'How was school today?' she'd say, 'Fine.' This gives her a way to talk to me without having to talk to me." Many parents would agree. One survey said that 63 percent of the parents questioned felt that using text messaging had improved communication with their children.

A WAY TO GUIDE Experts agree that today's kids live in a world very different from their parents'. Technology has taken kids with it but left many parents behind. There is far less interaction between kids and adults on a day-to-day basis. This leaves many teens feeling isolated. One eighth-grader said, "We're kind of like adults. We've learned how to run our own lives, think for ourselves, make decisions for ourselves."

The fact remains, though, that kids need the guidance that parents can give. Parents' involvement in their children's lives helps kids avoid harmful behavior. However, kids cannot get this guidance if they rarely talk to their parents. Although texting is not a **substitute** for face-to-face conversations in families, it can certainly help keep parents and kids feeling connected.

Communicating by using text messaging is a way to strengthen the important bond between parents and their children. That is a **victory** for both parents and kids.

THE DOWNSIDES Even though text messaging has a growing number of supporters, there are still some downsides. One big downside is the cost of sending the messages in the first place. In most cases, each message sent costs about 15 cents. That may not sound like much, but it quickly adds up. To most parents, though, it is worth the cost.

Another downside is that some parents are resistant to the idea of using text messaging and have a fear of miscommunication. However, there are online dictionaries that define many text messaging terms. Parents can use the dictionaries to learn the language of texting. The founder of one of these dictionaries says, "There's a bit of a fear factor." Some parents may not be as comfortable with technology as their kids are.

Whatever downsides there may be, text messaging is here to stay. As with other forms of technology, people will be more comfortable with using it as time goes on. Costs will also come down. Soon, even the most diehard opponent may find himself or herself tapping out this message: IMHO, txtmsg'ing is GR8!

WRAP IT UP

Find It on the Page

1. What are two reasons kids like text messages from parents?

2. What percentage of parents surveyed believed that text messaging improved their communication with their kids?

3. What are two benefits parents see with using text messaging to communicate with their kids?

Use Clues

4. Why might some parents dislike the idea of texting with their kids?

5. How would you encourage an adult to try text messaging?

6. What can we learn from the fact that many parents and other adults are using text messaging? Explain.

Connect to the Big Question

After reading the article, do you think that text messaging can be a way to help kids and adults communicate? Explain.

Real-Life Connection

Guilty or not guilty? Not all court cases end with a simple verdict, or result. Sometimes a verdict includes "by reason of insanity." Before reading the article, rate your knowledge of the insanity defense on a chart like the one below. Share with others what you know about these topics.

	Know a Lot	Know a Little	Know Nothing
Criminal justice system			
Insanity plea			
Moral responsibility			

WORD BANK

compromise (KAHM pruh myz) *noun*   When you reach a **compromise** with someone else, you both give up something you want in order to settle an argument.
EXAMPLE: *My teacher and I worked out a **compromise**. My homework will be a day late, but it will be complete.*

detect (di TEKT) *verb*   When you **detect** something, you notice its existence.
EXAMPLE: *Do you **detect** the smell of smoke in here?*

injury (INJ ree) *noun*   An **injury** is harm or damage done to someone or something.
EXAMPLE: *The bird could not fly because of its wing **injury**.*

negotiate (ni GOH shee ayt) *verb*   To **negotiate** with someone is to try to reach an agreement through discussion and compromise.
EXAMPLE: *Lia was able to **negotiate** with her mom to get a later curfew.*

stalemate (STAYL mayt) *noun*   A **stalemate** is a situation in which no further action can occur.
EXAMPLE: *Talks about which sports team would get new uniforms ended in a **stalemate**.*

Can all conflicts be resolved?

A man has committed a violent crime. In court, he says, "I didn't know what I was doing." His attorneys say the man committed the crime, but he should not be punished, because he is insane. What do you think? As you read the article, ask yourself: Is an insanity plea legitimate or just an excuse for criminals?

The Insanity Defense

At 1:30 P.M. on March 31, 1981, John Hinckley Jr. stepped from a crowd of onlookers and tried to kill Ronald Reagan, the president of the United States. Although he failed, he did cause **injury** to the president, a member of the president's staff, and law enforcement officers. The crime was committed in clear view of many people. There was no doubt that the young man had done the crime. However, at the end of his trial more than a year later, Hinckley was found not guilty by reason of insanity. Instead of prison, Hinckley was sent to a mental hospital, where he remains.

The verdict in Hinckley's case did more than irritate a few people. It kicked off a nationwide debate about whether people accused of a crime can claim they were insane when they did it. If they were capable of planning and then committing a crime, how could they later claim to have been insane? One starting point is to identify what *insane* means in a U.S. court of law.

▲ Judges may send convicted criminals to mental institutions instead of jail.

MORAL RESPONSIBILITY Very young children cannot be convicted of a crime if they do not know right from wrong, because they cannot be held morally responsible for their actions. For most people, moral responsibility comes with age and maturity. However, psychologists say that there are some adults who cannot recognize right from wrong. Since these adults cannot tell the difference, they should not be held morally responsible for their actions. In a U.S. court of law, an adult like this may be considered insane.

> Juries almost never acquit people by reason of insanity.

Hinckley was judged insane because psychologists determined that his mind was not functioning like a normal adult's. Like many other people who commit violent crimes, Hinckley was suffering from a severe mental illness. Hinckley's attorneys said that the mental illness prevented Hinckley from being responsible for his actions. He could not be punished, they said, if he really did not know what he was doing. Of course, since he did prove that he could commit a violent act, it was not safe to release him either. Instead, Hinckley's defense attorneys were able to **negotiate** a **compromise.** Hinckley would not spend the rest of his life in prison. However, he would be committed to a mental hospital, where he could be treated for his illness. The jury agreed.

NO EXCUSE People who are against the use of an insanity defense say that criminals like Hinckley do know what they are doing. Opponents of the insanity defense say that everyone who commits a serious crime like Hinckley's could be said to be mentally ill. Otherwise, the person would not commit the crime in the first place. There are many people who struggle with severe mental illness who do not commit crimes. These illnesses are treatable. They should not be used as an excuse for violent behavior.

Some states have another verdict: guilty but mentally ill. This verdict says that a criminal is mentally ill but still guilty. Criminals found not guilty by reason of insanity can often get treatment from doctors. Criminals found guilty but mentally ill may not get treatment. Some may get treatment, but if they are deemed to be cured, they will go to prison to serve the rest of their sentence.

People who support the insanity defense believe that mental illnesses are not always treatable. Psychologists and psychiatrists have been able to **detect** patterns of behavior. These mental **detectives** have gathered evidence that a person can be insane but seem normal. Hinckley and others with similar conditions suffer from delusions. These are ways of thinking that are completely apart from reality. Even though people with delusions may seem normal, the world does not appear to them as it does to other people. Therefore, experts say, such people cannot be held to the rules of behavior other people are held to. Their punishments should be **negotiable.**

LOW SUCCESS RATE Cases like Hinckley's capture the public's interest and spur debate. Often, that debate ends in a **stalemate,** with neither side giving in. The fact remains, though, that very few people who commit crimes use an insanity defense. An expert in public policy studied the use of the insanity defense. This defense was used in less than 1 percent of about 1 million cases. Of the cases in which it was used, only about .25 percent succeeded. The report concluded, "Juries almost never acquit people by reason of insanity."

WRAP IT UP

Find It on the Page

1. What crime did John Hinckley Jr. commit?

2. What kept Hinckley from receiving a guilty verdict and being sent to prison?

3. What is the argument against using the insanity defense?

Use Clues

4. What might happen if the insanity defense were not an option?

5. What conclusions can you draw from the fact that the insanity defense is not used very often?

6. How would you change the insanity defense laws to make them more effective?

Connect to the Big Question

After reading the article, do you think we should have the insanity plea as part of our legal defense system? Explain.

Real-Life Connection

You most likely use a locker to store items in school. Is that locker your own private place? Tell whether you agree or disagree with these statements. Explain why.

1. Students have the same right to privacy as adults.

2. School lockers are the property of the school.

3. Lockers should never be searched.

Check It Out

A search warrant is an order granted in court by a judge, usually to a law enforcement officer. The warrant gives law enforcement officers permission to enter private property and search for evidence of a crime.

WORD BANK

argument (AHR gyuh muhnt) *noun*   An **argument** is a reason or set of reasons for or against a point of view.
EXAMPLE: *I have no **argument** against recycling—I think it is a great idea.*

influence (IN floo uhns) *noun*   **Influence** is the effect that something has on a person or thing.
EXAMPLE: *My dad's **influence** helped shape my plans for after high school.*

irritate (IR uh tayt) *verb*   When you **irritate** someone, you annoy or anger the person.
EXAMPLE: *Sam's toe tapping is starting to **irritate** me.*

negotiate (ni GOH shee ayt) *verb*   To **negotiate** with someone is to try to reach an agreement through discussion and compromise.
EXAMPLE: *I hope to **negotiate** with my mom to get a bigger allowance.*

stalemate (STAYL mayt) *noun*   A **stalemate** is a situation in which no further action can occur.
EXAMPLE: *The brothers' disagreement ended in a **stalemate**, because neither one would admit the other might be right.*

Can all conflicts be resolved?

Like many students, you might store books, a coat, and things you consider private in your locker. Your locker might even be decorated inside to make it "yours." But is a locker really a student's space? As you read the article, ask yourself: **Should schools have the right to do random searches of student lockers?**

Privacy vs. Safety

Rushing to class, you realize you have left your textbook in your locker. You hurry back to your locker. As you round the corner, you come to a sudden stop. Your locker door is wide open, as are several others. Two teachers are standing there. It is clear they have been checking the contents of each locker. The sight does more than **irritate** you. You have done nothing wrong. Why were they looking in your locker? Does the school have the right to do this?

That question is being asked in one of the hottest debates in the United States today. In a random locker search, school officials can open any locker and examine its contents. To those who oppose such searches, the issue is about Americans' right to privacy. The Fourth Amendment to the U.S. Constitution states that no one has the right to search another's home, possessions, or person without a specific reason and a court-ordered warrant. People who oppose random searches **argue** that students in school should be protected by the Fourth Amendment.

PRIVATE AREAS Many students and adults see school lockers as students' private areas. A locker, they say, is personal space within the school community. A student needs this space, some people claim. It is a safe area into which no one can intrude without the student's permission. Respecting that privacy demonstrates adults' trust of kids.

Is your locker a private space?

For the vast majority of students, the desire to protect their privacy is totally harmless. They might use their lockers to store items such as CDs, notes, letters, or magazines. Such items are not illegal and do not threaten anyone, but a student may prefer that a teacher or another student not see them. There is the possibility, though, that some students are using lockers to hide things that *are* threats. This is a major concern, and it seems to support the **argument** that random searches are necessary.

SCHOOL OFFICIALS LOOK FOR LOCKER SOLUTIONS	
Type of Locker	How It Works
Clear Locker	Clear doors on lockers allow teachers and administrators to see items that students store in their lockers.
Smart Locker	Students open lockers with swipe cards instead of locks. School officials can lock down all the lockers at once. They can also monitor students' use of their lockers.

HIDDEN THREATS Illegal drugs are a real problem in many schools. Theft of personal items is also a problem. Thieves may use their lockers to store stolen goods, believing that lockers provide a safe hiding place. Weapons are the most serious threat. In the United States, more than 100,000 students bring guns to school every day. Each day, thousands of students and teachers are threatened with bodily harm. In one study, 57 percent of all public elementary and secondary school principals who responded reported that their schools had experienced one or more incidents of crime or violence. Ten percent of all public schools reported a serious or violent crime. Those in favor of random searches say they are a way to address these threats.

Schools have a clear responsibility to protect students. The law requires it. Schools must take reasonable measures to prevent students from bringing weapons or drugs into school. Young criminals with drugs or weapons stashed in their lockers can be a lethal **influence** on other students. When it comes to protecting all students, yielding the right to privacy may be the wisest action.

SCHOOL PROPERTY People in favor of random locker searches also **argue** that school lockers are not the private property of students. Lockers, they point out, belong to the school. Students are allowed to use lockers in the same way they are allowed to use other school property, such as library books or computers. Along with the privilege of locker use, these people argue, should go the knowledge that lockers can be searched at any time. This understanding should be considered a school rule.

When it comes to random searches of school lockers, both sides of the debate seem to have reached a **stalemate.** Both sides agree there seems to be very little room to **negotiate.** People who oppose random checks say that the right to privacy is not **negotiable.** Schools say you cannot **negotiate** the right to safety.

People who favor the right of schools to do some form of locker search seem to have been more **influential** than those who oppose it. Sam Davis is the dean of the University of Mississippi School of Law. He is also an expert on the constitutional rights of children. He says, "The court over the last fifteen to twenty years has really gone with preserving the government's interests over the individual's. There's really no question that students have fewer constitutional rights in a public school setting than they do outside."

WRAP IT UP

Find It on the Page

1. What is a random locker search?

2. List three things that random searches can help find.

3. Summarize the reasons for not performing random locker searches.

Use Clues

4. What effect might random locker searches have on students' feeling of safety within a school?

5. What actions rather than random searches could schools take to help ensure student safety?

6. What is your opinion of Sam Davis's statement that students have fewer constitutional rights in school than out of school? Explain.

Connect to the Big Question

After reading the article, how do you feel about random searches of student lockers? Do you think they are a violation of privacy? Explain.

Real-Life Connection

Think about what it means to be intelligent. Use a word web like the one below to capture your thoughts about intelligent people, the meaning of intelligence, and the best ways to measure intelligence.

Intelligence

Who is intelligent?

How do you measure intelligence?

What is intelligence?

WORD BANK

insecurity (in si KYOOR uh tee) *noun*   **Insecurity** refers to a lack of confidence.
EXAMPLE: *Shawna's insecurity disappeared when she realized she knew the answers to the test.*

method (ME thuhd) *noun*   A **method** is a way of doing something.
EXAMPLE: *My workout method keeps me in shape for playing sports.*

mislead (mis LEED) *verb*   When you **mislead** people, you give them the wrong idea about something.
EXAMPLE: *I did not try to mislead you about our homework. I did not know we had any.*

oppose (uh POHZ) *verb*   When you **oppose** something, you take a position against it.
EXAMPLE: *The citizens oppose having a landfill in their town.*

reaction (ree AK shuhn) *noun*   A **reaction** to something is the feeling it causes or the action taken in response.
EXAMPLE: *Cameron wanted to see his mother's reaction when she opened the gift.*

Can all conflicts be resolved?

Today is the day of an important test. Unfortunately, you feel very nervous. You are afraid that you will just freeze up, even though you know the answers to the questions. It does not seem fair that so much rides on one test! As you read the article, ask yourself: **Do standardized tests really measure what they are supposed to measure?**

The IQ Question

Have you ever taken an IQ test? If you live in the United States, you may have taken one when you began kindergarten or first grade. It is a special test that is intended to evaluate a person's ability to do certain things. These things include thinking, solving problems, analyzing situations, and remembering. How well you can do these things is supposed to predict how well you will do in school and in the workplace.

FIRST IQ TEST ATTEMPTS IQ tests were first developed in 1904 by a French psychologist named Alfred Binet. He came up with a **method** to determine a child's mental age in relation to actual age. The purpose of the test was to determine if a child might need extra help in school. Several years later, an American named Lewis Terman at Stanford University took Binet's work and built upon it. Terman used a formula to come up with a score called the intelligence quotient, or IQ. This score is calculated by dividing the tested mental age of a child by that child's actual age, then multiplying by 100. The IQ test became known as the Stanford-Binet test.

▲ Can an IQ test really predict your future success?

The Stanford-Binet test became the most widely used intelligence test in the United States. During World War I, the U.S. Army gave the test to 1.7 million soldiers coming into active service. They used test scores to determine what type of job the soldier should have. The Stanford-Binet test was used to evaluate schoolchildren during their first years in school. Some employers used IQ tests to decide who to hire.

RELIABLE? Eventually, there was a **reaction** to the popularity of the test. Some people began questioning whether these tests "worked." If the tests did not accurately measure intelligence, the results could **mislead** testers. Have you ever done poorly on a test because you had a cold or a headache? How about people who get nervous when taking tests? What if someone taking an IQ test just has a "bad test day"? A poor score could easily result in feelings of **insecurity** when it comes to school subjects. Students who have

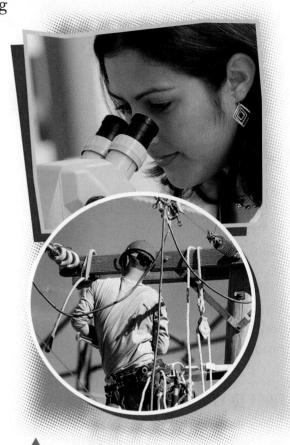

Experts have identified different kinds of intelligence.

low scores may become **insecure** or simply give up. A **misleading** IQ score could lead to a lifetime of just giving up.

WHAT IS INTELLIGENCE? Another problem with IQ tests is that it is not clear exactly what they can measure. As early as 1920, the famous journalist Walter Lippmann said, "We cannot measure intelligence when we have not defined it." More than eighty-five years later, the experts still cannot agree on a definition of intelligence. Is a person who cannot read well but is an expert at fixing machines not intelligent?

What about a physics professor who has a hard time holding a conversation? What about a doctor who has unhealthful habits? Is that person intelligent?

Those who **oppose** IQ tests point out that these tests are too limiting. The tests seem to measure only what people already know rather than their ability to learn new information. **Opponents** of current IQ tests say that there are many types of intelligence. Dr. Howard Gardner developed a theory of multiple intelligences. According to Gardner, there are eight different types of intelligence. A person could show abilities in one or more areas that far exceed the abilities of other people in his or her age group but not score well on a standard IQ test. Such a test can measure only a few of the eight types of intelligence identified by Gardner.

Even though there is controversy about IQ tests, some are still used. People who believe strongly in testing say that, when used properly, IQ tests do help identify students who may need extra help in school. The tests also help identify gifted students who can benefit from special programs that help such students meet their potential. The discussion about IQ testing is not likely to go away anytime soon. That there is discussion, though, seems to show that people are trying to make sure the tests are used in the right way.

WRAP IT UP

Find It on the Page

1. What does *IQ* stand for?

2. List two things that IQ tests have been used for.

3. Summarize the argument against IQ tests.

Use Clues

4. How might the information that a child has a very high IQ affect that child?

5. What other methods could be used to measure intelligence?

6. What is your opinion of standardized IQ tests, such as the Stanford-Binet? Explain.

Connect to the Big Question

After reading the article, how do you feel about standardized tests? What do you think they really measure?

Real-Life Connection

Many teenagers live in towns and cities that have curfew laws, which say young people cannot be in public places at certain times. Some adults and teenagers feel that curfew laws are unjust. Other adults and teens feel the laws serve an important purpose. What do you think the two sides of this argument might be? Make a pro and con table like the one shown below. Use it to write what you think people might say to support their views.

Teen Curfews Are Useful	Teen Curfews Are Not Useful

WORD BANK

cause (kawz) *verb*   To **cause** something to happen is to be the reason that it happens.
EXAMPLE: *Your untied shoelace might **cause** you to trip.*

oppose (uh POHZ) *verb*   When you **oppose** something, you take a position against it.
EXAMPLE: *We **oppose** cutting the music program to save money.*

reaction (ree AK shuhn) *noun*   A **reaction** to something is the feeling it causes or the action taken in response.
EXAMPLE: *When Lucia read the cartoon, her **reaction** was to laugh.*

solution (suh LOO shuhn) *noun*   A **solution** is an answer to a problem.
EXAMPLE: *Once I figured it out, the **solution** to the puzzle seemed simple.*

violence (VY luhns) *noun*   **Violence** is the use of physical force to harm someone or to damage property.
EXAMPLE: *The **violence** of the crowd resulted in broken store windows.*

THE BIG ?

Can all conflicts be resolved?

Many adults and law-enforcement professionals think, "Keep the kids off the streets during the night, and crime will go down." Others, though, say that teen curfews do not really do anything positive. They just restrict the rights of law-abiding teens. What do you think? As you read the article, ask yourself: **What do teen curfews accomplish?**

The Curfew Question

10:38

Your basketball game ran really late. Now you find yourself hurrying home down a dark street. Your mind is on the game. You do not even notice the car easing along the curb of the sidewalk until it stops right next to you. Your heart skips a beat because your first **reaction** is to be afraid. After all, it is late at night. Your second **reaction,** though, is surprise, because you recognize the car and driver. A police car has pulled up alongside you.

The police officer waves you over to the car, and you think, "Now what?" As soon as the thought crosses your mind, though, you also know the answer. Looking quickly at your watch, you realize that you are out on the street past curfew. Overtime at the game kept you too late.

Though you have a good reason for being out, you might still get a ticket. If you do, you or your parents will have to pay a fine.

▲ Curfew laws ensure that teens do not stay out too late.

Your parents know where you have been. They also know you are on your way home. You are not doing anything wrong. It is not your fault the game went into overtime. How is this fair?

CRIME TIME Scenes like this take place every day in thousands of U.S. towns and cities. One 1997 survey of the mayors of more than 300 major U.S. cities found that 80 percent of the cities had youth curfew laws. These laws state that kids under a particular age cannot be out of their homes during curfew times unless they are with an adult. The most common curfews are set for the hours between 10 P.M. and 6 A.M. Curfews usually affect kids seventeen years of age and younger.

The penalty for breaking curfew depends on where you live. In some cities, police will give you a warning and send you home. In other cities, curfew violators and their parents might get a fine of up to $500. Juveniles might be sentenced to do community service, and in some cases, parents might even face jail time.

Some crimes are committed at night, including many of those that involve **violence.** Officials in cities that have curfews claim that keeping kids off the streets at night reduces crime. One city reported a 50 percent decrease in juvenile crime after a curfew went into effect.

Supporters of curfew laws say that keeping kids off the street at certain times also protects law-abiding teens. Even though these teens might not **cause** trouble themselves, they could be the victims of gangs or one-on-one **violence.**

To many adults, the streets at night are no place for teens to be hanging out. A spokesperson for the Chicago Police Department has said, "If you're sixteen or younger, you belong in the house, not standing on a street corner."

PUNISHING THE WRONG PEOPLE Not everyone agrees that teens standing on a street corner are a source of crime or trouble. People who **oppose** curfew laws believe that such laws punish law-abiding teens. These are teens who may be coming home late from sports events, study groups, or other lawful activities. These teens may be taken to a police station and held there if they are out after curfew. Their parents will then have to come and get them and possibly pay a hefty fine. Curfew **opponents** say that this is punishment these law-abiding teens and their parents do not deserve.

Law-abiding teens may be paying the price for the few teens who break the law. One Chicago teenager says, "It's not fair. They think all kids are bad, but we're not."

The **opposition** also questions some of the research results. Some studies show that curfew laws have no effect on teen crime at all. Some people argue that teen crime seems to be going down because all crime across the United States is going down and not because of curfews.

Opponents say that curfews are not the **solution** to teen crime. Supervised evening activities and increased gun and drug control would go further to **solve** the problem of teen crime. These efforts would help prevent crime in the first place. Besides, they would be more just than curfews that restrict *everyone*.

WRAP IT UP

Find It on the Page

1. What are the most common city curfew hours?

2. List two reasons youth curfew opponents give for their opinion.

3. Which statements in the article support the idea that youth curfews help reduce teen crime?

Use Clues

4. How does each side in the curfew debate use the same data to support its views?

5. How would you change youth curfew laws to make them fairer to everyone? Explain.

6. Do you think youth curfew laws infringe on the rights of teenagers? Explain.

Connect to the Big Question

Do you think youth curfew laws help reduce the amount of crime committed by teenagers? Explain why or why not.

Real-Life Connection

You stop in at a local shop after school. As usual, you pick up some snacks and something to drink. When you pay for your purchases, you realize that the cashier has made a mistake and not charged you for a couple of items. What would you do in this situation, and why? Make a table like the one shown below, and use it to write your thoughts.

A cashier forgets to charge me for a few items.	
I would . . .	I would do this because . . .

WORD BANK

argument (AHR gyuh muhnt) *noun*   An **argument** is a reason or set of reasons for or against a point of view.
EXAMPLE: *Jen's **argument** for cooking at home was that eating out costs too much.*

interact (in tuhr AKT) *verb*   When you **interact** with people, you exchange information with them.
EXAMPLE: *Luis is a great clerk because he can **interact** with the store customers.*

introduce (in truh DOOS) *verb*   You **introduce** something when you bring it to a place, or cause it to be used, for the first time.
EXAMPLE: *Mr. Hanna decided to **introduce** the new algebra concept to his students slowly.*

victorious (vik TOHR ee uhs) *adjective*   A **victorious** person has won something, such as a contest or a race.
EXAMPLE: *The **victorious** players proudly accepted their trophy.*

viewpoint (VYOO poynt) *noun*   A **viewpoint** is the way a person looks at or thinks about something.
EXAMPLE: *Keith's **viewpoint** is that football is better than baseball.*

Can all conflicts be resolved?

A history teacher says, "Today, we are going to talk about honesty and integrity." The kids look confused. They thought today's class was going to be about the American Revolution. The teacher points out that character has a lot to do with history and life in general. As you read the article, ask yourself: **Should character be taught in school?**

Learning Character

You walk into class and sit down. No sooner does the class begin than your teacher passes out a sheet of paper. Oh, no! Pop quiz! Taking a closer look at it, though, you realize it is not really a pop quiz. It asks questions, but the questions are sort of odd.

You wonder what kind of test this is. Then, you learn it is not really a test but a way to help you start thinking about the choices you make every day. These choices help form your character. Your character defines the type of person you become. Some school systems believe that learning how to develop good character is as important to your education as everything else you study. They are putting this belief into practice through character education programs.

What would you think if your teacher gave you this test? ▼

CIRCLE THE ANSWER THAT BEST APPLIES

1. I can be counted on to do what I say I will do.	Never	Sometimes	Alw
2. I will tell a lie to avoid trouble.	Never	Sometimes	Alway
3. I admit if I do something wrong.	Never	Sometimes	Always
4. I make fun of people.	Never	Sometimes	Always
5. I do the right thing even if my friends don't agree.	Never	Sometimes	Always

STOP

CORE VALUES Character education programs use a number of different methods to **introduce** kids to the idea that character is important. Self-evaluation quizzes are one method to get kids thinking about character, and so are discussions and classroom activities that teach the importance of certain core values. These values usually include respect, honesty, responsibility, compassion, trustworthiness, and perseverance.

Schools that have **introduced** character education programs say that they have seen real changes. One study done in California showed that school attendance went up at the same time that suspensions from school went down. Parents, teachers, and students were found to have better attitudes about school in general. One woman remembers a character education program she took part in when she was a middle-school student in Ohio: "A lot of people changed." These results suggest that schools are on the right track in making character education part of their curriculum.

Some schools build character through service projects.

HOME, NOT SCHOOL Some people, though, offer the **argument** that school is not the proper place for teaching character. These people feel that character education is the responsibility of parents, not teachers. Teachers, they say, have enough to do in covering the regular academic subjects. Also, they ask, do values that define good character not differ from culture to culture? Are kids not being taught only one way of being a good person?

Steve Johnson is the director of character education at the Markkula Center for Applied Ethics at Santa Clara University in California. He offers the **viewpoint** that character is "not about being part of any culture; it's about being human. Whatever your background, culture, language, etc., you cannot be successful, you cannot run a society without human minimums in the way of conduct."

The challenges faced by today's kids are different from the challenges faced by kids of previous generations. One challenge for today's kids is that they simply do not spend as much time with parents and other adults as kids used to. Instead of learning about core values from parents, some kids are learning them from other kids. They are also learning values from the mass media. Supporters of character education believe that kids need to learn values from the adults in their lives. Johnson cites a 2002 survey to support this view: "Only 25 percent of the kids reported that adults talked with them about their personal values."

PARTNERSHIP Parents and other adults know that to teach good character values, they need to **interact** with kids more than they do. Schools recognize this as well. One solution is to give kids an **introduction** to character building through a partnership between the school character education program and the parents. Parents are getting involved in conveying the character concepts being taught in their kids' schools. The parents try to reinforce those concepts actively by being good role models for their kids.

Few people will **argue** that character education is not important. **Viewpoints** differ regarding where that education should come from, but everybody is **victorious** when kids get good character education. Character education has long-term benefits. It helps kids grow into adults who can successfully lead society into the future.

WRAP IT UP

Find It on the Page

1. What are two examples of core character values?

2. Which statements support the idea that character should be taught in schools?

3. How can parents help a school's character education efforts?

Use Clues

4. Why do schools want to teach character?

5. What might happen if schools did not teach character?

6. What is your opinion of Steve Johnson's statement that character does not depend on a particular culture, background, or language? Explain.

Connect to the Big Question

After reading the article, do you think that character should be taught in school? Explain.

 **Interview**

Answer the Big Question: Can all conflicts be resolved?
You have read about some debatable issues. Now, use what you learned to answer the Unit 2 Big Question (BQ).

STEP 1: Partner Up and Choose
Your first step is to pick Unit 2 articles that you like.
Get together. Find a partner to work with.
Read the list of articles. Discuss which articles listed on the left side of this page were the most interesting to you.
Choose two or more articles. Pick articles that you both agree on.

STEP 2: Reread and Answer the Unit BQ
Your next step is to answer the Unit BQ with your partner.
Reread the articles you chose. As you reread, think about the Unit BQ and whether conflicts can be resolved.
Answer questions. For each article you chose, ask your partner,

- What issue is this article about? What disagreements, or conflicts, do people have about this issue?
- Do you think these conflicts can be resolved? Why or why not?
- How does the information in this article help you answer the question: Can all conflicts be resolved?

Take notes. As your partner answers, take interview notes. Leave room for notes you will take in the next steps.

STEP 3: Discuss and Give Reasons
During this step, talk about your partner's Unit BQ answer.
Discuss the answer to the Unit BQ. Ask your partner to list reasons based on things he or she read in the articles:

- What details in the articles help you figure out whether all conflicts can be resolved?
- What makes some conflicts easy to solve? What makes others difficult?

Write your partner's answers. Add to your interview notes.

STEP 4: Add Examples

Now, finish the interview by asking for real-life examples.

Prompt your partner. To help your partner think even more deeply about the Unit BQ , say the following to your partner:

- Think about conflicts you have been involved in or ones you have heard or read about.
- Could they be resolved? Why or why not?

Add to your notes. Add your partner's examples to your interview notes. Be sure the notes have specific details.

STEP 5: Check and Fix

Next, you and your partner will look over the interview notes to see whether they could be improved.

Use the rubric. Use the questions on the right to evaluate your work. Answer each question yes or no. Then trade interview notes with your partner. Use the rubric to evaluate your partner's work.

Discuss your evaluations. Explain to your partner why you answered a question yes or no. For every no answer, explain what your partner could do to get a yes answer.

Improve your interview notes. If your interview notes could be improved, fix the mistakes or add details.

STEP 6: Practice and Present

Get ready to present your partner's views to your classmates.

Practice what you want to say. You will use your interview notes to explain how your partner answered the Unit BQ. Think about what you will say. Practice your presentation with your partner.

Present your interview notes. Introduce your partner to the class and explain how he or she answered the Unit 2 BQ. Include at least one specific example from an article and one from your partner's own experiences. You might want to use a multimedia tool to summarize your main points for your audience.

> ## RUBRIC
>
> **Do the interview notes . . .**
>
> - include an answer to the Unit BQ?
> - have the titles of at least two articles from Unit 2?
> - give at least one example from each article to explain the answer to the Unit BQ?
> - give at least one specific real-life example to explain the answer to the Unit BQ?

How much information is enough?

Have you ever heard the phrase "too much information"? Sometimes, all the information that we get can be overwhelming. How much do we really need to know? The articles in this unit explore the idea of information. As you read, figure out your own answer to the question of how much information is truly enough—and how much might be too much.

> Think of a time when you were overwhelmed by information about a subject. How did you decide which information to use and which to skip?

Real–Life Connection

Sometimes, kids get together to play in the park or on the playground after school. That is casual play. Other times, kids play sports in leagues or compete in tournaments or championships. That is organized sports. The two ways of playing can be very different. On a chart like the one shown, jot down words that come to your mind when you think about these different ways of playing. Use the examples to get started.

Casual Play	Organized Sports
pick-up game in the park	school basketball team

WORD BANK

challenge (CHA luhnj) *verb*   When you **challenge** someone's statements or decisions, you say the person is or might be wrong.
EXAMPLE: *Michele decided to **challenge** Luis's claims about what he could do.*

decision (di SI zhuhn) *noun*   When you make a **decision,** you choose one thing or course of action over another.
EXAMPLE: *There were so many cell phones to choose from that Inez had a difficult time making a **decision.***

development (di VE luhp muhnt) *noun*   When something undergoes **development,** it becomes bigger, fuller, or better.
EXAMPLE: *Because of her **development** as a public speaker over the past six months, Tracy won the speech contest.*

locate (LOH kayt) *verb*   When you **locate** an object, you find where it is.
EXAMPLE: *After looking all over his room, Ted was finally able to **locate** his glasses.*

valuable (VAL yuh buhl) *adjective*   Something that is **valuable** is worth a lot.
EXAMPLE: *Freddie learned a **valuable** lesson when he discovered that good friends make life better.*

How much information is enough?

Kids have always gotten together and played sports for fun. Over the years, however, youth sports have gotten more organized and serious. Adults are involved at every level, as coaches, trainers, organizers, and fans. As you read the article, ask yourself: How involved should adults be in youth sports?

Kids Just Want to Have Fun

Are you involved in more sports and having less fun? Some experts say that organized sports have started to lose something important: play. They also say that it may be adults who are spoiling the fun.

Of course, without adults, there would probably not be any organized sports for kids. The director of the Youth Sports Research Council at Rutgers University says, "Youth sports would cease to exist, if not for the significant contributions of parents who serve as coaches, officials, and league administrators." In other words, without adults, you can play a little soccer in the park, but you probably cannot **develop** an organized soccer league.

Actually, adults can offer more than just league **development.** They can teach **valuable** lessons about life and the rewards of hard work. They can also show how a good attitude helps make a person a good teammate. Adults do not always make sports better, however.

Kids play sports mostly to have fun.
▼

THAT IS MY KID OUT THERE! The problem is that some adults care only about winning. Everyone likes to win. When winning is the only thing that matters, however, play becomes work.

Adults who want only to win put too much pressure on young people. They tear down kids' confidence when they criticize them by saying things like, "When are you ever going to learn to dribble?" or "How many times do I have to tell you to relax?" The truth is that not everyone who plays a sport is going to be great at it. For example, most Little League baseball players are never going to play for the New York Yankees. Kids stop having fun when adults expect them to play like professionals or superstars.

Worse yet, some adults forget good sportsmanship. These adults **challenge** every **decision** the coach makes. They argue with referees and other game officials.

Research shows that the main reasons most kids play sports are to have fun and to be with their friends. In a recent poll, 1,228 students aged eight to eighteen were asked, "Which of the following would you prefer? Be on an organized sports team that wins a championship, but I don't get to play much. Be on an organized sports team that loses most of its games, but I get to play most of the time." The results (shown in the graph) suggest that most young people think playing is more important than winning.

Information is from Harris Interactive YouthQuery, July 2004.

THE TIGER WOODS QUESTION There is another side to this story, of course. Some star athletes, such as golf great Tiger Woods, say they owe much of their success to their parents. For example, Woods has said about his father, "I wouldn't be where I am today without him." Woods was not an average young athlete, however. From an early age, he showed strong natural ability. His father recognized young Tiger's ability and helped him **develop** it.

With competition so tough in the sports world, parents can make a big difference to a young athlete who has talent and drive. Some parents go without luxuries to pay for sports clinics for their kids. Others spend a lot of time and money to **locate** the best coach that they can for their children. These parents may travel hundreds of miles so that their kids can compete all over the United States.

Even if a young person is not headed for professional sports, early success in sports can bring important rewards. For example, many colleges give scholarships to promising young athletes. Some students need scholarships like these to pay for school. They cannot afford a college education any other way. Their parents know this, so they push a little harder for their kids to succeed in sports.

Adults must make a tough **decision** about youth sports. They need to **decide** whether their kids have special talents as athletes and how hard to push kids who do. Maybe the best thing adults can do is to remember that they are, above all, teachers. The lessons adults teach about playing sports will carry over into every part of kids' lives.

WRAP IT UP

Find It on the Page

1. What do some experts say is missing from organized sports?

2. According to the poll, what are the main reasons that kids play sports?

3. Contrast the attitude of kids who took the poll with the attitude of competitive parents.

Use Clues

4. What happens when parents care too much about winning?

5. How can people tell whether a young athlete is good enough to be a professional someday?

6. In your opinion, is it good for kids to play organized sports? Explain why or why not.

Connect to the Big Question

After reading the article, how involved do you think adults should be in youth sports? Explain why you feel as you do.

Real-Life Connection

Imagine this situation. You are at the park with some friends, having a good time. Your friends see a kid from school. He is new and does not yet fit in. One of your friends starts to bully the new kid, and the others join him. The new kid looks scared. What, if anything, would you do and why?

Check It Out

During World War II, about 6 million Jewish people were murdered by the government of Nazi Germany. This tragic event in world history is known as the Holocaust (HOH luh kawst). Most Jews died in killing centers or concentration camps. In some of the camps, Jews and other enemies of the Nazi government were forced to do slave labor. Most later died.

WORD BANK

discrimination (dis kri muh NAY shuhn) *noun*   **Discrimination** is treating people unfairly because they belong to a particular group.
EXAMPLE: *Discrimination against women kept them from voting in national elections until 1920, when women got the right to vote.*

global (GLOH buhl) *adjective*   Something that is **global** involves the whole world.
EXAMPLE: *World War I and World War II were global wars, because they affected countries all over the world.*

inequality (i ni KWAH luh tee) *noun*   **Inequality** exists when people are not treated the same or given the same rights.
EXAMPLE: *The seventh graders complained about the inequality of eighth graders having more rights and privileges.*

invariably (in VER ee uh blee) *adverb*   An event or a situation that happens **invariably** always happens.
EXAMPLE: *The sun invariably rises in the east and sets in the west.*

statistics (stuh TIS tiks) *noun*   **Statistics** are facts presented in the form of numbers.
EXAMPLE: *The statistics in Juanita's report showed that two out of three families in our city live in apartments rather than houses.*

How much information is enough?

During the Holocaust in Europe, millions of people did nothing to help save their Jewish neighbors. Not everyone refused to help, however. Some people risked their lives and their families to save the lives of Jews. What was different about those people? As you read the article, ask yourself: **What should we know about heroes of the past?**

Righteous Heroes

What kind of person would risk his or her own life and family to save other people from death? A religious leader? A doctor? A judge? What about a loser?

In the 1930s, Oskar Schindler was a middle-aged German man living in Czechoslovakia. He was not a success. In fact, many people would call him a loser. He started several businesses, but they **invariably** failed. He was not even a very good husband or father.

In 1937, Schindler joined the Nazi party. Adolf Hitler, leader of the Nazis, had promised to make Germany a **global** giant—the strongest country in the world. To do so, he planned to get rid of people who were not, in his opinion, "strong Germans." Under Hitler's leadership, the Nazis began a program of **discrimination** against many groups of people. Mostly, the Nazis **discriminated** against Jews. They closed Jewish stores, burned Jewish homes, and took Jewish lives.

▲ A Nazi soldier stands in front of a Jewish store in Berlin. The sign says, "Germans! Defend yourselves! Do not buy from Jews!"

UNLIKELY HERO After the Germans took over Poland, Schindler moved there. Schindler was given a factory in Krakow. A Jewish family had owned the factory. The Nazis, however, took over Jewish businesses and gave them to people who were not Jewish.

They believed these "gifts" would make people in other countries loyal to them, despite the terrible **inequality** in their treatment of Jews. The factory did not make Schindler loyal, however. He surprised many people by finding ways to save the lives of his Jewish employees.

His plan was to turn his employees into war workers. Schindler knew that the Nazis needed every war worker they could get. He hoped that if his Jewish employees made weapons for Germany, the Nazis would let those employees live. With this plan in mind, Schindler added weapons to the list of things his factory made. As he had hoped, the Nazis did not take his Jewish workers. Instead of herding them into a concentration camp or killing center—the almost **invariable** fate of Jews—the Nazis let them live so that they could work in Schindler's factory.

> Schindler said, "Don't worry; you are now with me."

Thanks to Schindler, more than a thousand Jewish workers and their families lived through the Holocaust. One of them, a woman named Helen Beck, said, "I will never forget the sight of Oskar Schindler standing in the doorway. I will never forget his voice: 'Don't worry; you are now with me.'"

ANOTHER UNLIKELY HERO Oskar Schindler was not the only person who worked against the Nazis. An eighteen-year-old nursing student named Irene Gut helped, too. She was living in Tarnapol, Poland, when the Nazis came. It was against the law to help Jews in Poland at that time, but Gut believed in a higher law.

A German army officer chose Gut to work for him in the buildings where he and his soldiers lived. Twelve Jews were forced to work in the laundry room there. When Gut saw that they had almost nothing to eat, she secretly brought them food.

Months later, she heard that all the Jews in Tarnapol were going to be murdered. By that time, she was working in the German officer's house. Gathering all her courage, she managed to hide the twelve Jews in his basement. **Statistics** show that the Nazis killed about 18,000 Jews in Tarnapol. The twelve Jews who worked in the laundry room, however, survived.

OTHERS WHO HELPED Many other ordinary people helped save the lives of Jews. Here are just a few of them.

Theodor Criveanu When the Nazis reached Czernowitz, Romania, 20,000 Jews were there. The Nazis planned to send them all to killing centers. Criveanu, a young officer in the Romanian army, which worked with the Nazis, handed out work permits. He knew that Jews with permits would probably be allowed to live. To save Jewish lives, he gave out more permits than he was supposed to.

Andrée Geulen-Herscovici As a young teacher, Geulen-Herscovici saw something that changed her life. She witnessed Nazis taking Jewish children from a school in Brussels, Belgium. She knew that the children would probably be murdered. Geulen-Herscovici spent the next two years hiding Jewish children in Christian homes.

Ruth Gruber The U.S. government sent Gruber to Europe on a secret mission to help bring a group of Jews to the United States. Gruber, then a young reporter, brought about a thousand Jews back.

These heroes are among almost 21,000 non-Jews who have been honored by the Yad Vashem Holocaust memorial in Israel. There, they are known as the Righteous Among Nations.

WRAP IT UP

Find It on the Page

1. Who was Oskar Schindler?

2. How did Schindler come to own a factory in Poland?

3. Briefly summarize how Schindler saved the lives of his Jewish factory workers.

Use Clues

4. Schindler became a hero to many people. What other examples of heroes can you find in the article?

5. Why do you think a teacher, like Andrée Geulen-Herscovici, would try to save children?

6. What would you say to the heroes described in the article if you could meet them?

Connect to the Big Question

After reading the article, how do you think learning about past heroes can help people today?

Real-Life Connection

Imagine that there are no statues. There are no murals, or wall paintings, on buildings, and there are no paintings in museums. Schools and libraries have no art on their walls, and street lights have no banners. Public buildings are all plain blocks with no color or decoration. The walls in subway stations are plain, with no bright tiles. Only people who can afford to buy art get to look at it. How would you feel? Jot down your ideas on a chart like the one below.

I would feel . . .	I would feel that way because . . .

WORD BANK

criteria (kry TIR ee uh) *noun*   Criteria are standards or tests that you can use to judge something.
EXAMPLE: *Marisol's **criteria** for a good pancake are taste, fluffiness, and a golden-brown color.*

decision (di SI zhuhn) *noun*   When you make a **decision,** you choose one thing or course of action over another.
EXAMPLE: *Jasmine has not yet made a **decision** about what she will wear to the school dance.*

exploration (ek spluh RAY shuhn) *noun*   When you do an **exploration,** you look at something carefully to learn about it.
EXAMPLE: *During my **exploration** of my new neighborhood, I found a good sports store with low prices.*

quality (KWAH luh tee) *noun*   The **quality** of something is how good it is.
EXAMPLE: *The best **quality** does not always cost the most money.*

quantity (KWAHN tuh tee) *noun*   A **quantity** is an amount.
EXAMPLE: *The little can holds only a small **quantity** of tuna.*

How much information is enough?

People do many things to make their world more beautiful and meaningful. They paint the walls of their houses and put up statues in the park. We all look at the art around us, but we do not always get to choose it. As you read the article, ask yourself: How much say should the public have in choosing public art?

THE PEOPLE'S ART

Should you get to choose the art you look at? Of course, you can probably choose the pictures that you put on the walls of your room. However, should you also get to choose the art that goes in the parks in your city? If people pay for art with their taxes, should they also set the **criteria** for **deciding** which art is chosen?

That question often comes up when people do not like a piece of public art. Most of the time, people are happy to see murals and statues and buildings that make the world more interesting. Other times, however, people complain about public art.

WHY PEOPLE COMPLAIN Social scientist Kim Babon says that most complaints about public art are not about their **quality** or even about the **criteria** used to make a **decision.** People complain when art in important public places is different from from what they expect.

For example, in 1967, many people in Chicago disliked a statue that was put in what is now Daley Plaza. The statue was designed by Pablo Picasso, a famous Spanish artist. Daley Plaza is an important public space, in the middle of the downtown. The statue was

▲
This colorful painting is a mural on one side of a public building.

placed in front of an important government building. On that site, people expected something more old-fashioned and dignified, like a statue of a general or a president. Instead, they got something that looks a little like a bird, a little like the Great Sphinx, and a little like an Afghan hound. It is also huge. The Chicago Picasso is 50 feet tall and weighs 162 tons. It cost a large **quantity** of money to make.

Although many Chicagoans were angry at first, they got used to the sculpture. Now, perhaps because people expect to see it, they like it. More than 40 years after the Picasso went up, Chicagoans take pride in it, and kids love to climb on it.

Chicagoans also like a piece of sculpture called *Cloud Gate,* in Millennium Park. The park was recently built in the heart of downtown Chicago. "It's an absolutely new space," says Babon. "There was nothing there. From the public's perspective, it could only get better." The park is near Lake Michigan, not a government building, so people did not expect anything in particular. They fell in love with the big, shiny sculpture that looks like a bean. In fact, "The Bean" is what many Chicagoans call it.

▲ Chicagoans and tourists alike enjoy looking at the shiny sculpture nicknamed "The Bean."

ART THAT SPEAKS FOR US . . . OR NOT People also get angry when public art seems to say something unpleasant about them. For example, some people criticize murals painted by young artists. These artists may use a mural as an **exploration** of neighborhood problems.

The murals show that life is not always easy. For example, some murals show different kinds of people struggling. Many people think that murals like these make their neighborhood look bad to other people. They say, "That's not what life is like here," and they want the murals painted over.

On the other hand, people who like the murals say they give a truer picture of their lives than do the statues in parks. Many of those statues were made a long time ago. Most show men from only one kind of background. In contrast, the murals show real life.

In the end, who is right? Who should **decide** which pieces of art belong in public places? We all have to look at public art, but not all of us are going to like every work that is put in a public place.

THE OPEN MUSEUM Maybe there is another way to think about public art. We could look at a city as a kind of open museum. When you **explore** a museum, you see lots of different paintings and statues. You like some of them. You do not like others. No one likes every single painting in any museum, just as no one likes every song on the radio or every show on television.

Maybe we could appreciate some of the public art we see and put up with art that we do not like. After all, public art belongs to the public, and the public is made up of many different kinds of people. We all learn to get along with one another, so maybe we can learn to get along with our public art.

WRAP IT UP

Find It on the Page

1. According to Kim Babon, what is the main reason people dislike some public art?

2. How did Chicagoans feel about the Picasso statue at first?

3. In Babon's opinion, why did Chicagoans like "The Bean" right from the start?

Use Clues

4. Why do you think cities put art in public places?

5. What criteria would you use to pick art for public places?

6. Think of a piece of public art in your neighborhood or city. In your opinion, is it good? Explain why or why not.

Connect to the Big Question

After reading the article, how much say do you think people should have in choosing public art for their community?

Real-Life Connection

What do you think this article will be about? Look at its title as well as its subheadings. Write them in a chart like the one shown. On the right side of the chart, write some notes on what you can tell about the article from previewing the title and subheadings.

Title:	Notes:
Subheadings:	

discrimination (dis kri muh NAY shuhn) *noun*   **Discrimination** is treating people unfairly because they belong to a particular group.
EXAMPLE: *During the 1960s, laws were passed to protect the rights of African Americans and end* **discrimination** *against them.*

explanation (ek spluh NAY shuhn) *noun*   When you give an **explanation** of something, you give details or reasons that help other people understand it.
EXAMPLE: *Thanks to Laurie's* **explanation** *of how to play the computer game, I was able to play and win.*

factor (FAK tuhr) *noun*   A **factor** is a cause or happening that helps bring about a result.
EXAMPLE: *Studying was an important* **factor** *in my getting a good grade on the test.*

point (poynt) *noun*   A **point** is an important idea or fact.
EXAMPLE: *The title of the article stated the main* **point***.*

reveal (ri VEEL) *verb*   When you show something that has been hidden, you **reveal** it.
EXAMPLE: *The magician lifted a scarf to* **reveal** *a beautiful bird.*

How much information is enough?

One way young people learn is to copy, or model themselves after, an adult. A good role model is an adult who sets a good example for kids. The role model might be a famous person, but he or she might also be a teacher, a family member, or a religious leader. As you read the article, ask yourself: What can I learn from a good role model?

Someone to Look Up To

What could you possibly learn about life from someone who is not like you? How could someone who has never been in your neighborhood teach you how to deal with gangs, bullies, or other problems? If you want to be a hip-hop musician, can you learn anything from a civil rights leader who lived and died before you were born?

We all choose people to model ourselves after. They may be athletes, singers, or other celebrities who have the kind of success we want. They may be leaders of causes in which we believe. On the other hand, they may be people in our families or in our communities who have values that inspire us. Our role models can be an important **factor** in the way our lives eventually turn out.

FAMILY ROLE MODELS Many famous people **reveal** that their role models are also their family members. From family, the celebrities learned values like courage, hard work, responsibility, and kindness.

Many young people look up to singer-actress Queen Latifah. ▶

These early influences are a **revealing explanation** of certain people's success. They may also help **explain** why some successful people remain good and kind to others.

Recording star Alicia Keys says that her role model was her mother. "Growing up, we didn't have anybody but each other to survive in the city. She really helped me to become the type of person I am; the strong-mindedness that I have is all because of her. . . . She taught me to stand on my own two feet."

American League baseball manager Jerry Manuel says his father was his role model. "When I was a youngster, I would come home and begin to try to tell my dad about what I had done in the game, but he would always cut me off and ask how the team did. It was not until I told him about the team that he would listen to anything I had to say about how well I had done." Manuel used this lesson to become a good leader whom his players respect and trust.

> Alicia Keys said her mother "taught me to stand on my own two feet."

TEACHERS AND COACHES Sometimes, adults at school and in sports are role models for young people. Edward James Olmos, a Latino actor, says his baseball coaches were important role models. Olmos calls them "tremendous mentors." From them, he says, he learned "discipline, determination, perseverance, patience—key ingredients that I still use today." Those values helped Olmos overcome **discrimination** to become a respected actor in Hollywood.

Zina Garrison also had a sports figure as a role model. Garrison was the second African American woman to reach the finals at Wimbledon, the famous tennis tournament in England. She says that her inspiration was Althea Gibson, the first African American woman to become a Wimbledon champion.

Garrison went to a tennis camp that Gibson had organized. At first, Garrison had a hard time at the camp. She was not doing well, and she was ready to quit. Then she had a talk with Gibson. As Garrison recalls, "She said I had to put everything on the line and not give up." Because of the talk, Garrison stayed and learned.

FAMOUS ROLE MODELS Television and the Internet are filled with stories about famous people. We read about what they say and do. Sometimes, we envy their success and money. It is therefore not surprising that we sometimes look up to these people as role models. Money and popularity are not always the best measures of success, however. Often, the best role models are rich in spirit and values rather than in dollars and cents.

One example is a role model Queen Latifah listened to. She says that Martin Luther King, Jr. inspired her when she worked at a fast-food restaurant. She explains, "Dr. King said that you must put 100 percent into everything you do, because it's not about the job, it's about the content of your character. . . . I was cleaning the filthiest bathrooms around. . . . But I cleaned those restrooms like they were in my home." Latifah understood the **point** King wanted to make. His words helped teach her a sense of determination that has made her a successful singer and actress.

Role models have helped many people be all they can be. The trick, of course, is to pick good role models. Whether or not your role models are famous, they should be people worth copying.

WRAP IT UP

Find It on the Page

1. Who was Alicia Keys's role model?

2. What did Keys learn from her role model?

3. Briefly summarize what Jerry Manuel learned from his father.

Use Clues

4. What can role models do for young people?

5. Who are your role models and why do you look up to these people?

6. Do you think the famous people described in the article had good role models? Explain.

Connect to the Big Question

After reading the article, what do you think you could learn from a role model? Explain your answer.

Real-Life Connection

You have probably used a computer to go on the Internet. Maybe you work on a computer in school, or maybe you have a computer at home.

In a word web like the one below, write what comes to mind when you think of the Internet.

Internet

fast

exploration (ek spluh RAY shuhn) *noun*   When you do an **exploration,** you look at something carefully to learn about it.
EXAMPLE: *Through careful research, I did a thorough **exploration** of the topic, learning as much about it as I could.*

quality (KWAH luh tee) *noun*   The **quality** of something is how good it is.
EXAMPLE: *The pizza at that restaurant costs a lot, but its **quality** is so good that it is worth the price.*

quantity (KWAHN tuh tee) *noun*   A **quantity** is an amount.
EXAMPLE: *I have to go to the store to buy some school supplies, because I have only a small **quantity** of notebook paper left.*

statistics (stuh TIS tiks) *noun*   **Statistics** are facts presented in the form of numbers.
EXAMPLE: ***Statistics** show that more drivers get in accidents after dark than during the day.*

How much information is enough?

The Internet gives you access to a huge amount of information. It seems as though you can find out almost anything you want by searching there. How good is the information you find, though? As you read the article, ask yourself: **Can we trust the information we find on the Internet?**

NET SMARTS

Quick! Which rock band made the best-selling album of all time? People have often had arguments about questions like this. Not long ago, to settle their arguments, they went to the library to find answers. If the library did not have the answers, people had to ask experts at schools, government agencies, newspapers, or magazines. By the time the experts answered, the question might not seem important or interesting anymore. (By the way, if you guessed that the Eagles made the best-selling album, you were right.)

Today we have the Internet. The Internet is a fast and easy way to answer fun questions, but what about the more serious ones? If you need good, up-to-date **statistics** for a school report, for example, can you trust the numbers that you find on the Internet?

QUANTITY OR QUALITY? Just a little **exploration** using a search engine will give you a huge **quantity** of Web sites to look at. Some of the sites may be of poor **quality,** however. Anyone can start a Web site and put up any kind of information on it. It is not against the law to post false information. You can claim that Mount Everest is in France, even though it is on the border between Nepal and Tibet.

Many students use the Internet to do research for school.

Because there is a lot of bad information on the Internet, it is wise to make sure the "facts" you find are actually facts. Use your Net smarts and ask good questions when you visit a site

WHO OWNS THIS? First, you should ask who owns the site. Some Web sites are owned by encyclopedia companies, newspapers, government agencies, and other information groups. These groups are more likely than others to try to get their facts right. They hire experts who check the information. As a result, you can probably trust the information on these sites.

To pick out good sites, look at Web addresses. A site is probably reliable if it has an address that ends in *.gov* (short for "government") or *.edu* (short for "education"). However, be careful of .edu sites written by students. Students may not be experts, and they may get their facts wrong.

Also, ask who wrote the pages on the site. Look for experts rather than companies with products to sell. For example, if you find information about a health topic, make sure the information comes from a doctor, a nurse, or a respected health group. If a site does not tell who the author is, look somewhere else for information.

▲
Make sure the statistics you get on the Internet are right.

WHERE DID STATISTICS COME FROM? Suppose a Web site claims, "More than 300,000 ice cream cones are sold every minute." **Statistical** statements like that may sound true, but are they? Look to see where the numbers come from. If a government group, such as the U.S. Department of Labor, provides a **statistic,** the number is probably right. Likewise, if a **statistic** comes from a university study, you can probably trust it. (Did you believe the ice-cream **statistic**? Though it may sound true, it is actually made up and therefore false.)

HOW OLD IS THE INFORMATION? Facts change. Old information may be wrong. Therefore, you need to make sure that the information you use is up-to-date. See whether a Web site tells when a page was put on the Internet. See whether a site tells when information was updated. Look also for statements with dates, like this one: "According to the 2000 U.S. census . . ."

When you have a lot of homework, you may feel like using the first Internet site you find. Doing that is risky, though, so use this shortcut instead. Go to a site that librarians have already **explored** for you. Look for homework help sites created by groups of librarians. Your school or public library may also have good databases, or collections of facts and sources of information, that you can search.

The Internet is a wonderful learning tool. You can use it to do research and learn more at any time. Just be sure to use your Net smarts. Weed out the bad sites and use only the good ones.

WRAP IT UP

Find It on the Page

1. What do *.gov* and *.edu* mean in a Web address?

2. Name two groups that are likely to give reliable statistics.

3. List three questions you can ask to see whether a Web site is reliable.

Use Clues

4. Why might old statistics no longer be correct?

5. What advice would you give to a student who is about to use the Internet for the first time?

6. Evaluate the ideas in the article. Do you think they will help you do better research on the Internet? Explain.

Connect to the Big Question

After reading the article, do you think you can trust information you find on the Internet? Explain why or why not.

Real-Life Connection

Are you ready to vote? To find out, write whether each of the statements below is true or false.

1. I know the name of my state senator.
2. I know three important problems our nation faces right now.
3. I know where to go to get information about candidates in an election.
4. I would vote in the next election if I had the right to.

Check It Out

People around the world have different ideas about when someone should be able to vote.

- Austria and Germany allow sixteen-year-olds to vote in city elections.
- Brazil and Serbia allow sixteen-year-olds to vote in all elections.
- The country of Liechtenstein does not let people vote until they are thirty.
- In Italy, a person has to be twenty-five to vote for senators.

accumulate (uh KYOO myuh layt) *verb*   When you **accumulate** something, you gather or collect it little by little.
EXAMPLE: *You can **accumulate** a lot of knowledge just by reading encyclopedia articles.*

derive (di RYV) *verb*   To **derive** is to get something from another source.
EXAMPLE: *Many of our traditions **derive** from European customs.*

global (GLOH buhl) *adjective*   Something that is **global** involves the whole world.
EXAMPLE: *Poverty and hunger are **global** problems that concern us all.*

inequality (i ni KWAH luh tee) *noun*   **Inequality** exists when people are not treated the same or given the same rights.
EXAMPLE: *Adela believed that **inequality** in the workplace kept her from getting promoted.*

How much information is enough?

When the United States was founded, only adult white males could vote. Since then, African Americans and women have gotten the right to vote. Is it time for younger people to be granted the right to vote, too? As you read the article, ask yourself: **At what age should a person be allowed to vote—sixteen or eighteen?**

Old Enough to Vote?

You have the right to work and pay taxes. Should you have the right to vote? Should a sixteen-year-old have the right to vote? People in countries around the world are asking about the voting age. It is a **global** issue. Some countries have already lowered the voting age, while others are considering it.

The United States is one of those countries. Some Americans question the law that says voters must be eighteen. The last time this kind of question was asked seriously was in the late 1960s, when the voting age was twenty-one.

At that time, the United States was fighting a war in Vietnam, a country in Southeast Asia. Eighteen-year-old soldiers fought and died in the war. Therefore, many people said the voting age should be eighteen. These people argued that someone old enough to die for the country is also old enough to vote for its leaders. To these people, there seemed to be a clear and basic **inequality.**

These young people are registering to vote. Once they are registered, they can vote in local and national elections.

In 1971, the United States passed the Twenty-sixth Amendment. It lowered the voting age from twenty-one to eighteen. Now, some people want to lower the voting age again.

YOUNG PEOPLE NEED A VOICE One reason that people give for lowering the voting age again is that young people need a voice in government. Lawmakers are making decisions that will affect the future—locally, nationally, and **globally.** The environment and health care are just two issues that may affect young people more than any other group. As young people grow older, they

> Many young people do not take the time to vote, even after they turn eighteen.

will have to pay for health care for older people who can no longer work. Moreover, young people may **derive** the most problems if the environment is dirty and unhealthful. The opinions of young people do not count, however, because they cannot yet vote.

A fourteen-year-old spoke to Minnesota lawmakers about voting rights: "If sixteen-year-olds are old enough to drink the water polluted by the industries you regulate, . . . then sixteen-year-olds are old enough to play a part in making them better."

Other people argue that teens will be able to have their say very soon. These people feel that the two years between the ages of sixteen and eighteen are not a long time to wait. These people point out that most citizens will have the right to vote for most of their lives. Moreover, many young people do not take the time to vote, even after they turn eighteen. People aged eighteen to twenty-four cast fewer votes than any other group in the United States, although that statistic may be changing.

YOUNG PEOPLE PAY TAXES Another reason that people give for lowering the voting age is taxes. Many young people begin working and paying taxes when they are sixteen. The United States was founded partly on the idea that taxation without representation is wrong. According to this idea, if you have to pay taxes, you should also have a say in who governs you, because the government spends your money and can raise and lower taxes.

Some people disagree. They say the taxation argument is equally true for people younger than sixteen. For example, people as young as age fourteen can work at some jobs. Fourteen-year-old workers have to pay taxes just as older workers do. Does that mean fourteen-year-olds should vote? Are they ready to vote? Do they know enough about government, and are they experienced enough to make important decisions about local, national, and world leaders?

WHO IS AN ADULT? That brings up the biggest question of all. When is a person an adult? It seems to be a simple question. Over the years, though, it has **accumulated** issues and exceptions. The law now says that people have to be a certain age to drink, to work, to get married, and to pay taxes. The age varies from one activity to the next. Moreover, "age laws" differ from state to state. Maybe, in the end, there is no final answer to the age question. Times change and people **accumulate** new views. Perhaps each new generation has to decide the answer for itself.

WRAP IT UP

Find It on the Page

1. How old does someone have to be in order to vote in the United States?

2. What was the main reason Americans had for lowering the voting age in 1971?

3. Briefly summarize the argument that young people should have the vote because they pay taxes.

Use Clues

4. Give a few other arguments for lowering the voting age.

5. Why do you think that many young people who can vote choose not to?

6. At what age do you think a person should be called an adult? Give your reasons.

Connect to the Big Question

After reading the article, at what age do you think a person should be allowed to vote—age sixteen or age eighteen? Explain your answer.

Real-Life Connection

Imagine this situation. You are walking past a shelter for stray animals. Through the window, you see a cage full of dogs, and you feel sorry for them. In fact, you are upset that no one is paying attention to them. You go inside the shelter and walk up to the woman behind the counter. "Those dogs need exercise," you say. "Yes," the woman replies, "but we need more helpers to exercise the dogs properly. Will you volunteer two hours a week?" What would you say? Jot down your thoughts on a chart like the one below.

Why I Would Volunteer	Why I Would Not Volunteer
I would because . . .	I would not because . . .

WORD BANK

challenge (CHA luhnj) *verb*   When you **challenge** someone's statements or decisions, you say the person is or might be wrong.
EXAMPLE: *Any time you say that hip-hop is bad, Nilda will **challenge** you.*

development (di VE luhp muhnt) *noun*   When something undergoes **development,** it becomes bigger, fuller, or better.
EXAMPLE: *The coach is happy with Paula's **development** as a batter.*

exploration (ek spluh RAY shuhn) *noun*   When you do an **exploration,** you look at something carefully to learn about it.
EXAMPLE: *Pedro watched his new cat's **exploration** of the house.*

valuable (VAL yuh buhl) *adjective*   Something that is **valuable** is worth a lot.
EXAMPLE: *My friends are among the most **valuable** things I have.*

How much information is enough?

Teenagers are very busy people. Besides doing homework, many teens also play sports or take part in other organized activities. Family life is important to many teens, too. As a result, some teenagers do not think that they have time to volunteer to help others. As you read the article, ask yourself: Can volunteering change teens' lives for the better?

Help Yourself and Others

You can learn a lot of **valuable** things in school. For example, you can learn math, science, English, and volunteerism. If you are not sure that last "subject" fits in with the others, you are not alone. Some people **challenge** the idea that volunteering, or doing helpful work without pay, should be a school requirement. Volunteer programs have always been around, but the idea that they should be required of students is a fairly recent **development.** What do teens get out of volunteering? Is it right to *make* them volunteer?

REQUIRING VOLUNTEERISM One state that requires young people to volunteer is Maryland. Before students can be graduated from a Maryland public high school, they must do seventy-five hours of volunteer work for their community. Popular volunteer activities include helping senior citizens, leading storytelling hours in day-care centers, and helping to clean local parks and streams.

▲ Helping senior citizens can be a satisfying volunteer activity.

The director of a Maryland student-service group believes the requirement is of **value** to teens and their community alike: "Teens get a lot of messages from the media and adults that they are not really part of the community, and are even sometimes viewed as a threat. Community service gives teens a way to be involved in their communities."

Maryland is not the only state that requires volunteer work of its students. School systems in New York, Connecticut, New Jersey, and North Carolina, among other states, have made volunteering a requirement. Virginia is also **exploring** the possibility, and other states are expected to follow.

BENEFITS OF VOLUNTEERING One of the strongest arguments in favor of the volunteering requirement is simple. If people start volunteering while they are still in school, they will **develop** a habit. They will continue to do volunteer service when they get older. That will help the country, because the government cannot pay for all the work necessary to help people in need.

Another argument for the volunteering requirement is that it is a practical form of career **exploration.** For example, teens who think they want to be teachers can volunteer to be teacher aides. Their volunteer work can help them decide whether teaching is right for them.

Studies have shown other benefits to volunteering. Students who volunteer feel more connected to their fellow students, their families, and their community. They get into less trouble. In addition, they achieve more both in and out of school.

VOLUNTEERING SHOULD BE VOLUNTARY Still, some people argue that volunteer work should be, well, voluntary. If schools require students to do community service, they say, should that service even be called volunteering? Does requiring the work take away some of its power?

What's more, some parents argue that it is their job to get their kids involved in community service. To make this point, the parents of a North Carolina high school student **challenged** the school's community-service requirement and sued the state. The court ruled that North Carolina has the right to set education requirements for children in public schools. The parents appealed the court's decision and tried to bring their case before the U.S. Supreme Court. However, that court turned down the case.

One study shows that volunteering in high school does encourage volunteering later in life. However, that finding holds true only if volunteering is not required. The study looked at the class of 1992. It asked students who did volunteer work why they did it. Eight years later, the study asked the same people again. More than half of all the people whose service was voluntary in high school were still volunteering. The people whose service was required in high school were volunteering at the same rate as those who had done no community service as students.

As more schools adopt the volunteering requirement, more people will probably accept it. Already, more than 10.6 million students have done community service as part of a school requirement.

WRAP IT UP

Find It on the Page

1. What is volunteering?

2. List three kinds of volunteer work that teenagers often do.

3. Briefly summarize how volunteering can help teens.

Use Clues

4. Why might volunteerism help the government save money?

5. Which volunteer activity noted in the article sounds the most interesting to you? Why?

6. In your opinion, should schools require students to do community service, or should the decision be left to parents and kids? Explain.

Connect to the Big Question

After reading the article, do you think volunteering can change teens' lives for the better? Explain.

Real-Life Connection

How do you feel about the information you get from the Internet, TV, and other sources? Find out by writing whether you agree or disagree with each statement below.

1. When I do research, I sometimes find a lot more information than I need.
2. Most of the information on the Internet is correct.
3. Movie stars are a good source of information about most topics.
4. It is impossible to learn too much.

Check It Out

Some experts say that we see and hear more information in one week than our great-grandparents received over their whole lives. This flood of information and the problems it can cause are called information overload. A main cause of information overload is the Internet.

WORD BANK

accumulate (uh KYOO myuh layt) *verb*　When you **accumulate** something, you gather or collect it little by little.
EXAMPLE: *Greta can **accumulate** more junk in a day than most people can in a year.*

explanation (ek spluh NAY shuhn) *noun*　When you give an **explanation** of something, you give details or reasons that help other people understand it.
EXAMPLE: *I was able to plant a tree correctly after I heard Alejo's **explanation** of the planting process.*

factor (FAK tuhr) *noun*　A **factor** is a cause or happening that helps bring about a result.
EXAMPLE: *The excellent head teacher at the karate school was one **factor** in my choice to go there.*

reveal (ri VEEL) *verb*　When you show something that has been hidden, you **reveal** it.
EXAMPLE: *Time will **reveal** that Juana was right.*

How much information is enough?

With the push of a few buttons or the turn of a page, you can find facts and opinions about almost any subject. For many of us, the question is not whether we have enough information but whether we have too much. As you read the article, ask yourself: Do I have information overload?

Too Much Information!

Can you get smarter and dumber at the same time? It could be happening to all of us, every day. That worries some experts on information technology. They **explain** that we have information overload, or access to more information than we can use well.

The main cause of information overload is the Internet. Even ten years ago, most people could not have imagined how much information would **accumulate** there. When you search for information about a topic, you may get a list of hundreds of sites to visit. Unfortunately, some of the sites may have wrong information. Anybody with a computer and a little know-how can put up a Web site. No one checks every fact on every site to make sure it is correct.

Personal sites, such as blogs, may also be listed as sources of information. These online diaries invite readers to give their opinions about topics. Readers often respond to blogs quickly, without giving much thought to what they write. Also, many people who respond to blogs are not experts. All the same, blogs are listed as sources of information alongside encyclopedia articles, newspaper stories, and other, more reliable sources of information.

▲ People can get information overload from the Internet.

How do you wade through all the sites and blogs to find good ones that have the information you need? One answer is to use information experts to go through the "facts" that people put out there. Librarians should probably be your main information experts. There are also research Web sites that list links with good information. Web masters have checked each link on these sites to make sure that it is useful.

PROFESSOR CELEBRITY Another kind of information overload is listening to too many different opinions. For example, we sometimes listen to the opinions of famous people, even when they are not experts on a subject. Television shows, newspapers, and celebrity magazines all **reveal** celebrities' opinions on everything from world news to psychiatry. Why do we listen to these opinions? There is a simple **explanation.** We already know who these famous people are. They already have our attention. As a result, they stand out from the crowd of people who want us to hear them.

▲ Watching too many news programs can also cause information overload.

Of course, actors and hip-hop stars have a right to their opinions, just like anyone else. They also have a right to give their opinions. It is up to us to decide whether to listen to them.

CAN YOU KNOW TOO MUCH? Some people worry that we actually take in too much information or that we can learn too much. In doing so, they misunderstand the idea of information overload. Learning is not a **factor** in information overload. If you really understand what you hear or see, it does not clutter your brain. It becomes part of who you are. However, you can spend too much time filling your brain and not enough time just living.

In a book on writing, Brenda Ueland advises, "Dare to be idle." She tells writers to do nothing sometimes. She calls it *moodling,* a word she made up from the words *mood* and *doodling.* Ueland believes that a person's imagination "needs moodling—long, inefficient, happy idling, dawdling and puttering."

The key word here is *imagination.* Life is more interesting and fun if you use your imagination. It is the source of art, music, stories, and video games. Almost everything that you really enjoy in life involves imagination—your own, someone else's, or both.

Besides, you cannot be truly smart without imagination. Imagination is what lets you find great new solutions to old problems. It helps you look at an **accumulation** of facts and see patterns and possibilities in them.

CAN INFORMATION HURT IMAGINATION? Information cannot kill your imagination. On the contrary, it can actually open your mind and feed your imagination. However, you do have to be smart about the information you see and hear. If you are thirsty, you do not go out and jump into a lake. You pour a glass of water. Likewise, if you need information, you do not look at every possible source. You pick the best. That way, you will never drown in facts.

WRAP IT UP

Find It on the Page

1. What is information overload?

2. What is a main cause of information overload?

3. Briefly explain why it is not possible to learn too much.

Use Clues

4. Why do people listen to the opinions of celebrities?

5. How would you solve the information overload problem?

6. In your opinion, is it important to feed your imagination? Explain why or why not.

Connect to the Big Question

After reading the article, do you think you have information overload? Explain.

PROJECT: TV Commercial

Answer the Big Question: How much information is enough?
You have read articles about information and how it affects people. Now, use what you learned to answer the Unit 3 Big Question (BQ).

STEP 1: Form a Group and Choose

Your first step is to pick Unit 3 articles that you like.

Get together. Find a small group to work with.

Read the list of articles. Discuss which articles listed on the left side of this page were the most interesting to you.

Choose two or more articles. Pick articles that you all agree on. Write the titles on separate pieces of paper for note taking.

STEP 2: Reread and Answer the Unit BQ

Your next step is to answer the Unit BQ with your group.

Reread the articles you chose. As you reread, think about the Unit BQ.

Answer questions. For each article you chose, answer these questions:

- What is this article about?
- According to the article, what kind of information might be "too much information"? What is really necessary and important for people to know?
- What do you think? How much information is enough?

Take notes. You will answer the Unit BQ in a TV commercial, "selling" your answer to viewers. Start brainstorming ideas.

STEP 3: Discuss and Give Reasons

During this step, discuss reasons that will help your group sell your Unit BQ answer to viewers.

Discuss your answer to the Unit BQ. Support your group's answer by giving reasons based on information in the articles and on your own experiences.

Summarize your reasons. Go over your notes and underline or circle ideas you want to include in the commercial.

STEP 4: Create Your Commercial

Now, make a final plan for your commercial.

Get a grabber. Think of the best way to grab your audience's attention. How will you make sure they are watching or listening?

Create a script for the commercial. Make sure each group member has a part in the commercial. Write a script—the words each group member will say. Think of ways you can convince your viewers about how much information is enough. You need to use language that will persuade them.

STEP 5: Check and Fix

Next, you and your group will check your commercial to make it even more convincing.

Use the rubric. Use the questions to evaluate your commercial script. It will be easier to evaluate if you read it aloud together.

Discuss your evaluations. If you answered no to any question, think of what you need to do to answer yes. If you need help from another group, listen to each other's commercial "practice" and answer the questions.

Improve your commercial. If your commercial could be more convincing or interesting, change the script so that audience members will "buy" your answer to the Unit BQ.

STEP 6: Practice and Present

Get ready to present your commercial.

Practice your commercial. Use your script to practice. You can write each person's part on a separate index card. Remember to use persuasive words and show enthusiasm.

Present your commercial. It is time to perform your commercial! If you have time and resources, think about shooting a video of your commercial to show the class. You can use music, special effects, and so on to help sell your idea in a convincing presentation.

> ### RUBRIC
>
> **Does the TV commercial . . .**
> - clearly answer the Unit BQ: How much information is enough?
> - include ideas from at least two Unit 3 articles?
> - have a lively and interesting script that will grab audience members' attention?
> - include persuasive language to "sell" your answer?

WHAT HE SAID UP THERE REALLY MADE SENSE.

HE DEFINITELY HAS MY VOTE!

UNIT 4

What is the secret to reaching someone with words?

The speaker's words were so powerful that they persuaded students to vote for him. What are the secrets of powerful speakers? In what other ways do we use words to reach people? In this unit, you will read about words used in rap, on billboards, in poetry slams, and in real-life adventures. Think about what makes these words powerful.

Think about something you read that had a great effect on you. What did you read? Why, do you think, was it so powerful?

Real-Life Connection

What are some ways that poetry and rap are similar? What are some ways that they are different? Jot down your ideas on a diagram like the one below.

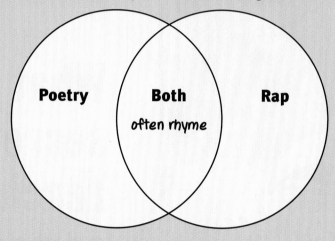

connection (kuh NEK shuhn) *noun*   A **connection** is a link or similarity between people or things.
EXAMPLE: *Shaquana feels a special **connection** with her cousin because they are family and they both like the same music.*

cultural (KUHLCH ruhl) *adjective*   Something that is **cultural** has to do with a particular group's beliefs, values, and customs.
EXAMPLE: *We celebrate many Mexican holidays because our **cultural** roots are in Mexico, my parents' birthplace.*

experience (ik SPIR ee uhns) *noun*   An **experience** is an event that you have lived through.
EXAMPLE: *Ron's favorite childhood **experience** was visiting his aunt.*

express (ik SPRES) *verb*   When you **express** an idea or a feeling, you put it into words, pictures, or actions.
EXAMPLE: *Tanya wants to **express** her feelings in a rap song.*

What is the secret to reaching someone with words?

Imagine two people listening to the radio. A rap comes on, and one says, "I cannot stand that noise!" The other says, "That is not noise. It is poetry set to music!" Who is right? As you read the article, ask yourself: **Is rap a form of poetry?**

RAPPING ABOUT POETRY

In the early 1970s, a new kind of music was brewing. It came from the streets of the Bronx, New York, not from recording studios. It was so new, it did not have a name. Still, everyone cool knew the music was hot. It had its roots in soul; the disco beat; new electric sounds; and the fast, smooth talk of deejays.

People in the music business know a moneymaker when they hear it, and music producer Sylvia Robinson was no exception. In the late 1970s, she gathered together Master Gee, Wonder Mike, and Big Bank Hank. The Sugarhill Gang was born. The group's 1979 hit single "Rapper's Delight" gave the music wings. The sound no longer belonged just to New York. Now, rap had a name, and it belonged to the whole world. It quickly became a **cultural** sensation. From rap grew a whole new youth **culture** that came to be called hip-hop.

People began to talk about rap as if it were poetry. Like poetry, it has rhythm, it often rhymes, and it **expresses** ideas in fresh, memorable ways. Does that mean that rap is a kind of poetry?

The Sugarhill Gang raps for club goers in 1979.

MAN, THAT **BEAT** MAKES ME MOVE MY **FEET**!

STORIES WITH A BEAT There is nothing new about making words rhyme or speaking them with a beat. People have been doing it for thousands of years. The great stories of ancient **cultures**—from the Greek *Odyssey* to the Anglo-Saxon *Beowulf*—were in the form of poems. Long before these stories were written down, they were told face-to-face. Storytellers told them in the great halls of kings and in the smoky huts of poor people. Rhythm and rhyme helped the tellers remember the stories. Vivid descriptions made the stories fun to hear.

Likewise, African storytellers used rhythm to tell the histories of their villages. When Africans were enslaved and brought to America, they brought with them the tradition of telling stories to a beat. Rap takes these African **cultural** roots and combines them with American music styles to create a modern sound.

> Rap has helped make poetry popular with young people again.

RAP AS POETRY To many people, that modern sound is a kind of poetry. In fact, some say rap has helped make poetry popular with young people again. Like poetry, rap paints pictures with words, and it tries to **express** deep feelings about life. Moreover, many rappers, like many poets, draw on their own **experience** when they write. Doing that can make rap as personal as a poem can be.

Newspaper writer Caryn James is one of the people who sees a **connection** between poetry and rap. "Rap is street poetry," she wrote in a review of a TV show. She went on to say that rap is a "vibrant, essential, and growing means of **self-expression.** [Rappers] blur the line between literature and pop **culture.**"

THE RAP AGAINST RAP Other people do not believe that rap is poetry. For example, a Harvard professor said, "I make a distinction between verse and poetry." His point is that a rap is more like a greeting-card verse than it is like a poem. **Expressing** a similar view, a former president of the American Academy of Poets called all spoken-word poetry a "karaoke of the written word." In his opinion, rap is an empty imitation of real poetry. He thinks that real poetry is meant to be read, not performed. Even some people who believe that rap is a form of poetry have complaints about it.

One objection is that rap insults women. *Essence* magazine, for one, is trying to stop negative images of women in rap. For some people, however, the magazine's efforts have come too late. One female reader wrote, "I just stopped waiting for the next song, the one that wouldn't insult me, bring me down, or just plain hurt. It never seemed to come. So I stopped listening to hip-hop stations, bit by bit." Another complaint against rap is that much of it contains swearwords and other offensive language.

In defense of rap, a professor points out that other kinds of music say negative things and contain offensive words. "Yet we focus on the black artists," she says, "not on the rockers and not even the white executives who are making big money from this kind of music."

There are other complaints about rap. Some people say that it focuses too much on violence. Of course, not all rappers write about violence, paint negative pictures of women, or use offensive language. Many rappers use clean language to say positive things.

Rap started out describing life on the streets. Like poetry, it amped up the intensity and range of its listeners' **experiences.** A strong **connection** with its audience will stay key to its success.

WRAP IT UP

Find It on the Page

1. Where did rap music start?

2. List three complaints that people have made against rap.

3. Compare and contrast rap and poetry. In what ways are they similar? Different?

Use Clues

4. Why do rappers use rhythm, rhyme, and other poetic devices?

5. Do you enjoy rap? Explain why or why not.

6. In your opinion, does this article do a good job of defining *rap*? Explain.

Connect to the Big Question

After reading the article, do you think that rap is poetry? Why or why not?

KICK IT OFF   Fit to a Tee

Real-Life Connection

What do you know about free speech and dress codes in schools? To find out, tell whether each statement below is true or false.

1. U.S. law gives you the right to say what you want anywhere you want.
2. It is against the law to keep students from wearing T-shirts with slogans, or sayings, to school.
3. Students have the right to talk about their political beliefs in school.
4. The U.S. courts have ruled that school dress codes are legal.

Check It Out

In most places, the school board decides whether public schools in the community have dress codes. The community elects school board members. Therefore, voters can help shape school rules by voting for people whose opinions they support.

WORD BANK

benefit (BE nuh fit) *noun*   A **benefit** is something good that results from an action.
EXAMPLE: *Better health is a **benefit** of exercise.*

individuality (in duh vi juh WA luh tee) *noun*   **Individuality** is all the qualities that make one person or thing different from another.
EXAMPLE: *Keely shows her **individuality** in the unusual clothes and jewelry that she wears.*

inform (in FAWRM) *verb*   When you **inform** someone of something, you give the person knowledge of it.
EXAMPLE: *My school said it will **inform** us about the dress code.*

meaningful (MEE ning fuhl) *adjective*   When something is **meaningful,** it is important and filled with significance and purpose.
EXAMPLE: *Marina said that graduation day was one of the most **meaningful** days of her life.*

THE BIG ?

What is the secret to reaching someone with words?

Do you have a T-shirt with a slogan on it? In many places, students cannot wear T-shirts like that to school. Some people say that school dress codes, or rules about clothing, unfairly limit what kids can wear and express. As you read the article, ask yourself: Where should we draw the line on freedom of speech?

FIT TO A TEE

Recently, a fifteen-year-old student in the southwestern United States was told to leave school because of his T-shirt. On his shirt was the name of a politician running for office. The dress rules at the student's school **inform** students that they can wear only certain kinds of T-shirts. Shirts with political slogans are not on the list. The student's father was upset by the rule. The father said, "It's a First Amendment Constitutional right, . . . and I don't know why he should give it up." Was the father correct?

FREE SPEECH—MOSTLY The First Amendment to the U.S. Constitution states that "Congress shall make no law . . . abridging freedom of speech." In simple words, that **means** the government cannot pass laws that take away people's right to speak their mind.

The courts have stated, however, that schools can limit free speech for certain reasons. One reason is safety. Most schools do not let students wear gang colors or symbols to school. The court system usually gives the OK to rules like that, because they are **meant** to protect students from gangs. Similarly, most schools do not allow clothes with slogans that encourage bad habits, like drinking alcoholic beverages or smoking. That rule is **meant** to protect students' health.

At many schools, wearing slogan T-shirts is against the rules. T-shirts like the one this teen is wearing are usually OK.

A school can also set certain rules to make sure that all students have equal rights. Protecting equal rights includes giving different opinions an equal chance to be expressed. In other words, schools cannot let one student give opinions without letting students who disagree give their opinions. To make sure that all students' views are respected, many schools limit what T-shirts can express. (See the table for more **information** about dress codes.)

STRONG ARGUMENTS In the case of the student with the political T-shirt, the school had strong arguments to support its actions. The school pointed out that it had taken the time to **inform** parents and students about the dress code before the school year started. As a result, the school felt that the T-shirt rule should not have taken the student or his parents by surprise.

ITEMS MANY DRESS CODES BAN
Slogan T-shirts
Baggy pants
Gang colors
Midriff-exposing tops
Short skirts
Tight clothes

The school board added that the student had many other **meaningful** ways to express his opinions in school. The board wrote that students can "express themselves through the wearing of buttons, jewelry, or other symbols; forming a school-sponsored club; and speaking at limited public forum opportunities during the day." The principal of the school even offered to help the student start a school-sponsored political club.

This story has a happy ending. The student and his father worked with the school district to iron out their disagreement. Many other people still object to dress codes, however.

BREAK THE CODE OR SAVE IT? People against school dress codes say the codes do not respect **individuality.** These people argue that students should be allowed to express themselves in school. The teen years, they say, are a time when people learn who they truly are. Trying different styles of dress is part of the learning process.

People who support school dress codes reply that there are more **meaningful** ways for students to learn who they are. Kids can join school clubs, play school sports, or take part in school volunteer activities. It is better to build self-knowledge in these ways than through fashion, they argue. Moreover, these people say, a **benefit** of dress codes is that they encourage good behavior. These people say kids tend to act more grown-up when they dress more grown-up.

HARD TO WRITE Though people disagree about school dress codes, nearly everyone agrees that such codes are hard to write. No matter how fair schools try to be, people still complain. Take, for example, a dress code in a Virginia school. It banned clothes with pictures of weapons. When a student wore a shirt that showed men with guns, the school told him to leave. The student and his parents took the school to court, and a judge decided the dress code was too general. He pointed out that the code would ban clothes with the state seal of Virginia, which shows a woman holding a spear.

Whether you think dress codes are bad or **beneficial,** they are probably here to stay. About two of every five public schools have a dress code, and more schools will probably join them.

WRAP IT UP

Find It on the Page

1. Which amendment to the U.S. Constitution protects the right to free speech?

2. Identify two reasons that schools ban certain items of clothing.

3. Briefly summarize people's arguments against dress codes.

Use Clues

4. Find an example of a time when a judge ruled against a school dress code.

5. How do you think the United States would change if Americans lost their right to free speech?

6. In your opinion, are dress codes good, bad, or somewhere in between? Explain.

Connect to the Big Question

After reading the article, where do you think we should draw the line on freedom of speech?

Real-Life Connection

What do you know about the advertising technique called "spam"? Rate your knowledge on a chart like the one below.

Idea	Know a Lot	Know a Little	Know Nothing
What spam is			
Why companies use it			
How people feel about it			

WORD BANK

connection (kuh NEK shuhn) *noun*   A **connection** is a link or similarity between people or things.
EXAMPLE: *We learned that there is a clear **connection** between what we eat and how we feel.*

media (MEE dee uh) *noun*   The **media** are radio, television, the Internet, newspapers, and all other forms of communication that reach large audiences.
EXAMPLE: *The **media** reported on the movie star's wedding.*

relevant (RE luh vuhnt) *adjective*   When something is **relevant** to a topic, it helps make a point about the topic.
EXAMPLE: *My teacher said I should leave out ideas that are not **relevant** to the main idea of my speech.*

sensory (SENS ree) *adjective*   Something that is **sensory** has to do with one or more of the five senses.
EXAMPLE: *Dwanna says that the three-cheese pizza her father makes is a **sensory** delight.*

What is the secret to reaching someone with words?

Think about how many ads you see when you walk down a city street. Count billboards, ads on trains and buses, store ads, and any other ads you see. In just a few blocks, you might see more than a hundred ads. As you read the article, ask yourself: How do big-city advertising techniques affect us?

City

They are all around you. Towering ads on the sides of skyscrapers tell you what to wear, what to watch, what to eat. Ads for magazines whiz by you on buses. Giant screens flash brand names, products, symbols, and slogans. All are forms of urban (city) spam, and they are enough to give you **sensory** overload.

Like the e-mail spam they are named after, these outdoor ads try to get your attention, whether or not you want to give it. In fact, companies that use urban spam worry that their messages might get lost in the crowd of other messages. As one ad expert put it, "The more **media** messages we get, the fewer we listen to." As a result, advertisers look for ways to make their message stand out. One way is to make their ads look as if they are not ads.

LIGHT SHOWS How do companies make their ads look like something else? One way is to use pictures rather than words. Take, for example, the displays that a TV network used to advertise a new cartoon show.

Times Square, in New York City, is filled with urban spam.
▼

The network hired video artists to make light displays of a character from the show. The displays were placed on busy bridges and freeways so that many people would see them.

At first, the ads seemed like a great success. At night, when the displays were lit up, people could see the cartoon character from miles away. However, during the day, when they were not lit, the displays looked like strange metal boxes with wires sticking out. In one city, drivers thought one of the metal boxes was a bomb. The drivers used their cell phones to call police, and part of the city was closed while police investigated. That was the end of that spam.

STREET PAINTINGS AND MOVIES Another kind of "non-ad" looks like graffiti—writings or drawings made on walls or other surfaces likely to be seen by the public. Advertisers know that graffiti is popular with some young people. To make a personal **connection** with kids, the advertisers use a style of art that kids like. The graffiti-style ads show young people having fun using a product. A company advertised an electronic game system this way. Though the ad's message was not put into words, it was easy to **sense:** Buy the game system, and you, too, will have fun.

Another kind of outdoor ad is more like a movie. This type of ad is shown on giant screens, on sidewalks, or on the sides of buildings. Ads are projected onto these large flat surfaces to get people's attention. People cannot help noticing these monster ads, but the attention is sometimes negative. As one blogger put it, "Who thinks that by . . . sticking a picture and a text line in my nose, that I didn't choose or aim to get, I am going to get a positive attitude about the brand?"

> **People cannot help noticing these monster ads, but the attention is sometimes negative.**

STOP SPAM The truth is that many people are tired of city spam. They wonder whether private companies should have the right to use public spaces, like walls and sidewalks, to sell their products. Huge outdoor ads are commonly put in neighborhoods where people live. People who live in neighborhoods with spam complain that the ads do not benefit them in any way. These people point out that advertisers pay to rent advertising space in the neighborhood, but the money goes to building owners or to the city. It does not go to the average person who lives near the spam-filled streets.

Moreover, city spam sometimes advertises unhealthful products, such as liquor, in styles that are aimed at young people. Many people object to these ads. Parents do not want their kids to see ads like that every day on the way to school.

SAVE THE SPAM On the other hand, there are people who enjoy and **connect** with city spam. They think that spam is fun and interesting. When ads are **relevant** to their needs, people even find them useful.

Maybe a person wants to find the nearest fast-food restaurant, or maybe an adult in search of a birthday present for a teen wonders what to buy. Outdoor ads can provide information that the person wants.

Should spam be stopped, or should it stay? Maybe it should be up to the people who have to look at it, rather than the people who make money from it.

WRAP IT UP

Find It on the Page

1. What is city spam?

2. List three examples of advertising that could be considered city spam.

3. Briefly summarize arguments for and against city spam.

Use Clues

4. What do you think would happen if all ads were banned for a year?

5. If you ran your city, what rules would you set about outdoor advertising?

6. What kind of advertising is most effective in making you want to buy a product or service? Why?

Connect to the Big Question

After reading the article, how do you think big-city advertising techniques affect us?

Real-Life Connection

Imagine that you have a friend who likes to take risks. He does dangerous tricks on his skateboard, and he secretly hangs out with kids who are much older than he is. You are worried that your friend will get hurt or in trouble. What, if anything, would you say to him?

Check It Out

Chris McCandless was a young man from a rich family when he left home. He traveled to Alaska, where he went to live alone in the wilderness. *Into the Wild,* a book about him, has been made into a movie with the same title.

feedback (FEED bak) *noun*   When you give **feedback,** you tell or show your response to something.
EXAMPLE: *The audience's loud and enthusiastic clapping was all the **feedback** the chorus needed to know it had sung well.*

misunderstand (mi suhn duhr STAND) *verb*   When you **misunderstand** someone, you get the wrong idea about what the person meant.
EXAMPLE: *My mom and I sometimes **misunderstand** each other.*

reveal (ri VEEL) *verb*   When you show something that has been hidden, you **reveal** it.
EXAMPLE: *My grandmother opened the box to **reveal** a beautiful necklace.*

significance (sig NI fi kuhns) *noun*   The **significance** of something is the thing that makes it important or meaningful.
EXAMPLE: *My grandparents' fiftieth wedding anniversary had great **significance** for my family.*

valid (VA luhd) *adjective*   To be **valid** is to be based on truth or on fact.
EXAMPLE: *My teacher said that all the reasons in my paper were **valid** because they could be proven to be true.*

What is the secret to reaching someone with words?

Have you ever wanted something from life that family and friends seemed unable to understand? If so, then you may understand how Chris McCandless felt. He left a comfortable life behind to live in the Alaskan wilderness. As you read the article, ask yourself: Why has the story of Chris McCandless sparked controversy?

Alone in Alaska

You might say Chris McCandless had it made. He came from a wealthy family, and he earned a college degree, with honors. McCandless was unhappy, however. He thought that his life was too planned out. He longed for freedom and adventure.

Soon after college, in 1990, McCandless decided to start a new life. He left home without saying goodbye to his parents, brothers, or sisters. He gave himself a new name. He also gave away all the money he had saved and burned the money in his wallet. Then he hit the road to find adventure.

IN SEARCH OF EXPERIENCE For the next two years, McCandless wandered the western United States in search of interesting experiences. He worked in the wheat fields of South Dakota, and he flipped burgers in Nevada. When possible, however, he did not work. He said he did not want life to be about making money.

▲

In his journal, Chris McCandless wrote about his experiences and kept photographs of himself.

McCandless wanted to live off the land. He found deep **significance** in the beauty of nature, which he often talked to strangers about. He had a deep effect on many of them. Strangers did not stay strangers for long, because McCandless made friends easily.

THE ALASKA ADVENTURE In April 1992, McCandless hitchhiked to Alaska to live alone in the wilderness. He planned to live by his wits and not much else. McCandless packed light. About all he brought with him were a ten-pound bag of rice, a rifle, a homemade sleeping bag, and a pair of boots given to him by a stranger who gave him a ride to Denali National Park.

▲ This picture was taken in Denali National Park, where Chris McCandless journeyed.

Once McCandless was in the wilderness, he wrote his thoughts in a journal. He set up camp in an empty bus that someone had left twenty-two miles from the nearest road. He hunted and ate squirrels and birds, and he also gathered and ate plants and berries.

McCandless believed that his dreams of adventure and freedom were coming true. He explained in his journal that he was "no longer to be poisoned by civilization. He flees, and walks alone upon the land to become lost in the wild." He signed the journal "Alexander Supertramp." Then something went horribly wrong. In September, some hunters found his body. McCandless had starved to death. He was twenty-four years old.

FOOL OR SAINT? Some people think that McCandless was foolish to go live in the wilderness. People who have lived there, for example, say that he was too inexperienced to go it alone and that he should have brought more supplies. An Alaskan park ranger summed up an idea that many people find **valid:** "What [McCandless] did wasn't even particularly daring—just stupid, tragic, and inconsiderate."

Other people are fascinated by McCandless's story. One of these people is author John Krakauer. He read the young man's journal, talked to his family, and retraced his steps. In the book *Into the Wild*, Krakauer hoped to **reveal** what McCandless was like. The **feedback** about McCandless that Krakauer got from his friends on the road was very different from the picture the park ranger gave.

For starters, McCandless did have outdoor survival skills. For example, he knew how to fish and hunt. Krakauer says, "He was rash, untutored in the ways of the backcountry, and incautious to the point of foolhardiness. But he wasn't incompetent." Krakauer does not think that the way McCandless died **invalidates** the life he lived or the principles he tried to live up to.

To Krakauer, McCandless was an unusual young man on a spiritual quest, not a fool. Krakauer insists that McCandless did not **misunderstand** what he was getting into, nor did he underestimate the power of nature. In Krakauer's opinion, McCandless's main mistake was overestimating his own strength. "Were it not for one or two seemingly **insignificant** blunders," Krakauer wrote, "he would have walked out of the woods in August."

WRAP IT UP

Find It on the Page

1. Who was Chris McCandless?

2. How did he die?

3. Briefly summarize why McCandless went alone into the Alaskan wilderness.

Use Clues

4. Why might a park ranger be especially upset about McCandless's lack of preparation for the trip?

5. What would you do differently from what McCandless did if you planned to live in the wilderness when you were twenty-four?

6. In your opinion, was McCandless a hero or just a misguided young man?

Connect to the Big Question

After reading the article, give your opinion about why McCandless's story sparked controversy.

Real-Life Connection

What do you know about poetry slams? Rate your knowledge on a chart like the one below.

Idea	Know a Lot	Know a Little	Know Nothing
What poetry slams are			
Who the major performers are			
Why slams are so popular			

Check It Out

There are different explanations of why poetry slams are called "slams." The term may refer to a grand slam in baseball (a home run with the bases loaded). It may refer to a grand slam in a card game (winning all the tricks in one hand). It may refer to slam dancing, a style of dancing that was popular among punk rockers. It may refer to slamming the stage, which some poets do to emphasize their words.

WORD BANK

benefit (BE nuh fit) *noun*   A **benefit** is something good that results from an action.
  EXAMPLE: *Improved grades are a **benefit** of studying hard.*

cultural (KUHLCH ruhl) *adjective*   Something that is **cultural** has to do with a particular group's beliefs, values, and customs.
  EXAMPLE: *On our school's **cultural** exchange day, students honor their roots with special foods, songs, and dances.*

meaningful (MEE ning fuhl) *adjective*   When something is **meaningful,** it is important and filled with significance and purpose.
  EXAMPLE: *Andy's poem is **meaningful** to me because it describes exactly how it feels to win a big game.*

media (MEE dee uh) *noun*   The **media** are radio, television, the Internet, newspapers, and all other forms of communication that reach large audiences.
  EXAMPLE: *The **media** sent reporters to the scene of the big fire.*

THE BIG ? — What is the secret to reaching someone with words?

Imagine going out with friends to a coffeehouse. While you sip your soft drink, a kid your age gets up on stage and starts talking. You get caught up in what he has to say, and somehow he makes you feel what he feels. As you read the article, ask yourself: Why are poetry slams so popular?

Performing Poets

"When she was crying, I was crying. Raw passion was on stage, surging from the face, hers. Her body became her vessel; she smacked my brain across the face."

That was an audience member's reaction to a poem written and performed by a contestant at the Teen Poetry Slam championships in New York City in 2005. The audience member's reaction shows one important **benefit** of poetry slams. They are performance art that emphasizes raw, exciting emotion. As a result, they reach out to listeners and make them react.

YOU BE THE JUDGE Slam poetry is a **cultural** phenomenon. It is performance poetry for a competitive **culture.** In fact, some people feel that slam poetry is the perfect combination of art and sports. Here is how a slam works. A host chooses judges from among audience members who have come to watch the competition. At some slams, no one knows ahead of time who will perform. People volunteer to perform their poems when they come to the competition. For other slams, performers sign up ahead of time.

After each poet performs, the judges give scores. The poets who score highest perform another poem. Audiences boo poets whose work they do not like—or judges whose scores they disagree with.

This young woman is performing a poem at a slam. ▼

One popular slam is held at the Starry Plough in Berkeley, California. There, anyone can get up on stage and contribute a **meaningful** poem. The host, Charles Ellick, says, "Every single person has a story. You just never know who is going to come up and blow your mind with the depth of their soul."

Slam poetry probably started at a Chicago jazz club in 1984. The host of the slam was a construction worker named Marc Smith. He may have been inspired by the Nuyorican Poets Café in New York City, which has been holding spoken-word poetry contests for more than thirty years. Poetry slams caught on with the public, and by the late 1980s, they were being held around the country. In a few more years, poetry slams went global.

> **Poetry slams caught on, and by the late 1980s, they were being held around the country.**

AN EVENT FOR ALL MEDIA Poetry slams became even more popular thanks to hip-hop executive Russell Simmons. He brought slam **culture** to the broadcast **media.** He started a series on cable TV that hosted famous poets like Nikki Giovanni, Ise Lyfe, Jesus Papuleto Melendez, and Sonia Sanchez.

Simmons also published a collection of poems performed on cable TV. The editor of the poetry collection, Tony Medina, says, "This is our mouth on paper, our hearts on our sleeves, our refusal to shut up and swallow our silence."

A stage version of the show had nine performers celebrating their neighborhoods, backgrounds, and experiences. It opened in San Francisco in 2002. Then it moved on to Broadway, where it won a Tony Award. After that, the show toured Europe, where it was a **cross-cultural** hit with audiences.

Another poetry-slam show, hosted by Mos Def, began on cable TV in 2001. On the show, both well-known and lesser-known poets performed their work for a live audience. Musicians who are not thought of as poets appeared on the show. They included Lauryn Hill, Wyclef Jean, Alicia Keys, and Kanye West.

THE DOWNBEAT Not everyone who likes poetry likes poetry slams. Some people have voiced concern about shows that emphasize the performers' fame over their writing talent.

Poet Veronica Bonahan's mixed emotions are typical. She finds it **beneficial** that TV programs offer opportunities to poets. However, she also worries that slams will "dumb down the art form." Other poets say they will not participate in shows that highlight performance over content. These poets believe that the performance aspect of poetry slams cheapens the art form.

Moreover, some poets do not like the competitive nature of slams. They point out that poets may have something important to say but might be afraid to brave the scoring or the audience's high-octane reactions. This may be especially true of young, inexperienced poets who would like to take the stage. They may be scared off by the thought of being criticized in public.

On the other hand, getting involved in slams can build young people's courage. Before, says one teenaged poet, "I had no confidence in my intelligence. Now, this Sunday, I'm getting up in front of 20,000 people to read what I wrote."

WRAP IT UP

Find It on the Page

1. What is a poetry slam?

2. According to the article, where did poetry slams probably start?

3. Briefly summarize what happens at a poetry slam.

Use Clues

4. How is a poetry slam a combination of art and sports?

5. Would you go to a poetry slam if you could? Explain why or why not.

6. Do you agree that poetry slams dumb down the art of poetry? Explain.

Connect to the Big Question

After reading the article, why, do you think, are poetry slams so popular with young audiences?

Real-Life Connection

What do you think this article will be about? Look at the title of the article as well as its headings. Write them in a chart like the one below. In the box on the right, jot down notes on what you can tell about the article from previewing the title and headings.

Title:	Notes:
Headings:	

inform (in FAWRM) *verb*   When you **inform** someone of something, you give the person knowledge of it.
EXAMPLE: *The news programs on the radio **inform** us when our school closes because of bad weather.*

relevant (RE luh vuhnt) *adjective*   When something is **relevant** to a topic, it helps make a point about the topic.
EXAMPLE: *As I planned my paper, my sister helped me choose reasons that were **relevant** to the main idea.*

signal (SIG nuhl) *noun*   A **signal** is a sign of something to come.
EXAMPLE: *When the leaves fall from the trees, it is a **signal** that fall is here.*

valid (VA luhd) *adjective*   To be **valid** is to be based on truth or on fact.
EXAMPLE: *Tom's argument that air travel is unsafe is not **valid,** because statistics show that it is a very safe form of travel.*

What is the secret to reaching someone with words?

In a big country like the United States, people come from various backgrounds. Consequently, not every holiday seems important to everyone. As you read the article, ask yourself: **Who should decide which holidays we celebrate?**

It's a Holiday

Picture yourself, your friends, and your family on the Fourth of July. Maybe you are outdoors on a hot afternoon, enjoying a barbecue. Maybe you are waiting for the sun to set, a **signal** that fireworks will soon begin. Just about everyone knows why the Fourth of July is a holiday. It is our nation's birthday. Fewer people are sure about why we celebrate other holidays, such as Labor Day.

States decide which holidays to celebrate. Although there is some disagreement among states, most states close schools and businesses for at least ten major holidays.

A LONG TIME COMING Sometimes, it takes a long time for a holiday to become official. For example, Memorial Day was first celebrated on May 30, 1868. The purpose of the day was to honor soldiers who had died in the Civil War. However, more than a hundred years passed before Congress made Memorial Day a national, federal holiday.

Columbus Day was first held in 1792, but it did not become an official holiday until 1892 when President Harrison made it a national holiday. Though the holiday was not controversial at the time, it is now.

A crowd enjoys fireworks on the Fourth of July.

Some people are against the holiday, because they think it is impossible for anyone to "discover" a land where people have already been living for thousands of years. To show how they feel, these people call the holiday Native American Day or Indigenous Peoples Day. These names are a way of **signaling** that the land belonged to Native Americans long before Europeans arrived.

MARTIN LUTHER KING DAY

It also took awhile for Martin Luther King Day to become a federal holiday. King, an African American who led a nonviolent struggle for civil rights, was shot dead in 1968. Four days after he died, Congressman John Conyers introduced a bill that would make King's birthday a national holiday. Throughout the 1970s, people debated the issue. Some people thought no one civil rights leader should be singled out for such a significant honor.

OFFICIAL U.S. HOLIDAYS	
Holidays	Official Date of Holiday
New Year's Day	January 1
Birthday of Martin Luther King Jr.	January, third Monday
Washington's Birthday	February, third Monday
Memorial Day	May, last Monday
Independence Day	July 4
Labor Day	September, first Monday
Columbus Day	October, second Monday
Veterans Day	November, second Monday
Thanksgiving	November, fourth Thursday
Christmas Day	December 25

Information is from U.S. National Archives, "2008 Federal Holidays."

In the early 1980s, eighteen years after King's death, 6 million citizens signed petitions to make January 15, King's birthday, a national holiday. Congress supported the bill. Finally, President Reagan named the Monday closest to King's birthday a federal holiday. On January 20, 1986, people across the country celebrated the first official Martin Luther King Day. (For **information** about when official holidays are celebrated, see the chart.)

HOLIDAYS OF THE FUTURE?

Certain holidays are still debated today. Some people want to start a new holiday to honor Americans killed in the terrorist attacks on September 11, 2001. Other people feel that starting a new holiday would be unfair. They point out that we do not have holidays to mourn victims of the Holocaust, the Oklahoma City bombing, or Hurricane Katrina. Japan attacked the United States at

Pearl Harbor on December 7, 1941. Even this day, on which many lost their lives, is not commemorated by a national holiday.

There is also a movement to make election day a national holiday called Democracy Day. People in favor of the holiday hope that more people will vote, and take time to become **informed** about the issues, if they have the day off from work. One poll found that more than 60 percent of people in our country want to make election day a holiday.

Who should decide whether there should be a new national holiday? Right now, the public has a say, but that does not mean the people's say is final. If a group of people wants to add a new national holiday, that group usually gathers signatures from thousands of supporters. Then it has to **inform** a congressperson or senator of its wishes. After that, the government official introduces a bill that must pass both the U.S. House of Representatives and the Senate. If the president approves the bill, it becomes **valid.**

Would you like more holidays, or do you believe there are enough **relevant** holidays already? As you can see, it is not quick or easy to make a new official holiday!

WRAP IT UP

Find It on the Page

1. What groups decide which holidays to celebrate?

2. List the ten federal holidays celebrated in the United States.

3. Explain why some people celebrate Native American Day rather than Columbus Day.

Use Clues

4. Why are most federal holidays celebrated on Mondays?

5. What person or event do you think should be recognized with a new holiday? Why?

6. In your opinion, would more people vote on election day if it were a holiday? Explain.

Connect to the Big Question

After reading the article, who do you think should decide which holidays we celebrate?

Real-Life Connection

Imagine this situation. At home, you are having a private telephone conversation with a friend about a secret. A sister or brother overhears the conversation. Later, at dinner, he or she blurts out your secret to the rest of the family. What would you do in this situation, and why? Jot down your thoughts on a chart like the one below.

What I Would Do	Why I Would Do It

feedback (FEED bak) *noun*   When you give **feedback,** you tell or show your response to something.
EXAMPLE: *The coach gave Ellen **feedback** about the way she played to help her improve her game.*

individuality (in duh vi juh WA luh tee) *noun*   **Individuality** is all the qualities that make one person or thing different from another.
EXAMPLE: *Ranelle's parents were surprised by how different she was from her brother, but now they appreciate her **individuality.***

misunderstand (mi suhn duhr STAND) *verb*   When you **misunderstand** someone, you get the wrong idea about what the person meant.
EXAMPLE: *Javier hates it when his brothers **misunderstand** him.*

significance (sig NI fi kuhns) *noun*   The **significance** of something is the thing that makes it important or meaningful.
EXAMPLE: *A high school diploma has great **significance** because a person must usually have one to get a job or to go to college.*

What is the secret to reaching someone with words?

For some kids, siblings—brothers or sisters—are their role models. For other kids, siblings seem like their bitter enemies. Either way, the relationship between siblings is usually intense. As you read the article, ask yourself: How do siblings influence one another?

My Brother and Sister Drive Me CRAZY!

Y ou try to escape from them, but they are always there—arguing with you, telling you what to do, using your things, or prying into your business. Everyone who has at least one brother or sister knows that living with siblings can be hard. Is there anything good about having a brother or sister around?

Many studies suggest that there is. These studies found that siblings influence one another, and the effect often has great **significance.** Siblings help shape one another's personality. They teach one another how to end disagreements—and in some cases, how not to. Some siblings protect one another. Some siblings see the good in one another's **individuality,** and some always seem to **misunderstand** one another.

SOCIALIZING SIBS One reason that siblings influence one another so much is that they spend a lot of time together. In fact, one study found that most eleven-year-olds spend more free time with their siblings than with their friends, with their parents, or by themselves. On average, teenagers spend at least ten hours per week with their brothers and sisters.

Though siblings love one other, they often find it hard to get along. ▶

GIVE AND TAKE All that togetherness can help siblings learn how to get along with other people. "Siblings have a socializing effect on each other," says one psychologist. "Unlike a relationship with friends, you're stuck with your sibs. You learn to negotiate things day to day." In other words, you learn to give a little and take a little to get along with one another.

Of course, togetherness can also lead to disagreements and **misunderstandings,** but these can also teach you how to get along. In working out disagreements with siblings, you can learn **significant** conflict-resolution skills. Experts say that if you have practiced these skills with siblings, you will probably have more friends and get along

▲
Justin Upton, whose baseball-playing brother BJ is his role model, bats against the Los Angeles Dodgers.

well with classmates. Conflict-resolution skills can also carry over into your adult life, in which they can improve your relationships with friends, a spouse, and co-workers.

BENEFITS OF COMPETITION We all know that siblings often compete against one another. They may challenge one another physically, or they may try to win arguments with one another. They may also compete to be the "best child"—the one that Mom or Dad holds up as a good example. When competition goes too far, it can lead to hurt feelings. However, competition can also make you stronger. You may learn how to defend yourself, but you may also learn how to compromise without hurting someone else.

In their book *Siblings Without Rivalry,* Adele Faber and Elaine Mazlish pointed out another possible benefit of competition: achievement. Siblings who do well in or out of school can inspire you to work harder and achieve more than you would otherwise.

INTRODUCTION TO LIFE Older siblings can provide good advice and **feedback.** Unfortunately, they can also lead the way down the wrong path—to drinking, smoking, or other risky behaviors. In other cases, however, they set good examples. Even older siblings who make bad choices can have a good influence. Their younger sibs may see what can go wrong and decide to do just the opposite.

Having an older sibling of the opposite sex can be a great opportunity to learn and grow. If you are a girl, shooting hoops with your older brother can build your confidence in yourself. If you are a boy, seeing your older sister's sensitivity toward others can help you become a good listener.

"I don't **understand** how people learn to live in the world if they haven't had siblings," wrote author Anna Quindlen about her childhood. "They were my universe, even more than my parents."

Finally, when it comes time to date, girls with older brothers and boys with older sisters may feel less nervous. They may not find the opposite sex as confusing or mysterious as they would otherwise. They are used to talking with people of the opposite sex, and they can draw on conflict-resolution skills that they have learned at home.

WRAP IT UP

Find It on the Page

1. What are siblings?

2. List four skills kids can learn from living with siblings—skills they can use as adults.

3. Briefly summarize some ways in which siblings may compete with one another.

Use Clues

4. In your opinion, why do siblings often compete?

5. How would you advise a friend whose little brother or sister will not stop bothering your friend?

6. Do you agree that siblings can learn negotiating skills from one another? Explain.

Connect to the Big Question

After reading the article, in what ways do you think siblings influence one another?

Real-Life Connection

What do you know about what writing can do for your health? Writing from the heart can have positive effects on people who have the courage to be honest with themselves. Fill out a chart like the one below to examine the changes that creative writing can bring to people's lives.

How Writing Can Help		
Starting Out	Write About it	Afterward
feel sad		feel better
feel scared		feel more confident

WORD BANK

experience (ik SPIR ee uhns) *noun*   An **experience** is an event that you have lived through.
EXAMPLE: *To understand the older people in her neighborhood, Naomi drew on her **experience** of living with her grandmother.*

express (ik SPRES) *verb*   When you **express** an idea or a feeling, you put it into words, pictures, or actions.
EXAMPLE: *William plans to **express** his opinion of the movie in a movie review for the school newspaper.*

measure (ME zhuhr) *verb*   When you **measure** something, you figure out its size.
EXAMPLE: *One way we **measure** the success of our after-school program is to see how many students attend it.*

sensory (SENS ree) *adjective*   Something that is **sensory** has to do with one or more of the five senses.
EXAMPLE: *The many beautiful sights and aromas made my trip to the garden a **sensory** experience.*

What is the secret to reaching someone with words?

At the age of sixteen, Luis J. Rodriguez was on drugs, in a gang, and in jail. What would it take to turn around a life so troubled? He started reading and then writing poetry. Today, Rodriguez is a professional writer. As you read the article, ask yourself: **How can words change people?**

Writing That Heals

Because you are a student, you already know some good reasons to write. You write to complete assignments for school. You probably write to communicate in e-mail messages to friends or notes to your mom. You may also write letters to keep up with friends who have moved away, or maybe you write to **express** your opinion about an issue you care about. You may agree that writing can be important, but did you know that it can save lives?

RUNAWAY WITH WORDS Many programs for troubled young people have found that creative writing can inspire kids and help them turn their lives around. Take, for example, Runaway with Words, a poetry workshop for at-risk young people. A professor and a graduate of Florida State University started the workshop in 1991. They held the first workshop at a shelter in Panama City, Florida. The shelter provided a safe place for runaways as well as teens who have been abandoned. The people who ran the shelter wanted to help the teens talk about their problems and feelings. That way, the shelter staff would have a clearer idea of how to assist the kids.

For some teens, writing about themselves was easier than talking. It turned out that they had a lot to **express**.

A young woman reflects on her life. ▶

They discovered that writing was a good way to give **expression** to their feelings. They wrote about tough subjects, such as poverty, racism, anger, guilt, fear, and love.

Runaway with Words is now a nationwide program of poetry workshops. Over the years, thousands of kids have learned that putting their feelings into words helps them deal with a painful **experience.** Young people have also learned new writing skills, such as how to create **sensory** descriptions. These skills help the young writers gain control over their emotions. "This program changes lives," says one teacher.

▲
This young man is working to improve his reading skills.

A Runaway with Words workshop has also been started for kids who have been expelled from school. Many of these young people have been charged with crimes. If they are convicted, they will be sent to juvenile detention centers, or prisons.

A **measurement** of the young people's reading skills is taken before and after they take the Runaway with Words workshop. Because of the workshop, most of them improve their ability to read. Many of them also stop having problems with the law. Writing helps them learn ways other than violence to deal with their problems.

STREET POETS, INC. Another organization that uses writing workshops to reach troubled teens is Street Poets, Inc. It helps kids in the juvenile prisons, schools, and streets of Los Angeles County. The organization teaches kids to use increased self-awareness to break the cycle of violence in their lives.

The workshop leader describes the teens he teaches: "They are victims and perpetrators, addicts and dealers, schemers and dreamers. And once you get past the surface, they are desperate to find a way out of the self-destructive lifestyles they've chosen." The leader creates a safe space where the young writers can take risks and write the truth about their lives. In eight years of working with rival gang members, the leader says, a fight has never broken out in a workshop. One **measure** of success is that graduates of the writing workshops have gone on to teach the workshops themselves. Some graduates also have performed their poetry in schools.

WRITERSCORPS Getting at-risk and low-income kids excited about the written and spoken word is the main goal of WritersCorps. This program, founded in 1994, has reached thousands of kids in New York City, San Francisco, and Washington, D.C. The program published a book called *Same Difference: Young Writers on Race,* which features the poetry of kids from ages six to twenty-one.

Creative writing helps these young poets feel connected to their communities. Reading their work in front of groups also builds their confidence. Participating in poetry slams channels their competitive impulses in productive ways.

"Teaching kids to write is the most powerful way I feel I can affect their lives," says one poetry teacher. "I've seen writing help kids in profound ways." That is truly writing that heals.

WRAP IT UP

Find It on the Page

1. What is the Runaway with Words program?

2. Where did the Runaway with Words program begin?

3. Compare and contrast the Street Poets, Inc., and WritersCorps projects.

Use Clues

4. How do the risks that kids take in a writing workshop compare with the risks they take if they join a gang?

5. How would you test whether a writing workshop actually helped kids improve their reading skills?

6. In your opinion, are writing workshops the best way to help troubled kids? Explain.

Connect to the Big Question

After reading the article, do you think words can change people? Why or why not?

UNIT 4 WRAP UP

 **Graphic Organizer**

Answer the Big Question: What is the secret to reaching someone with words?

You have read about different ways people use words. Now, use what you learned to answer the Unit 4 Big Question (BQ).

STEP 1: Partner Up and Choose

Your first step is to pick Unit 4 articles that you like.

Get together. Find a partner to work with.

Read the list of articles. Discuss which articles listed on the left side of this page were the most interesting to you.

Choose two or more articles. Pick articles that you both agree on and each write the titles on your Unit 4 BQ graphic organizer.

STEP 2: Reread and Answer the Unit Big Question

Your next step is to answer the Unit BQ with your partner.

Reread the articles you chose. As you reread, think about the Unit BQ.

Answer questions. For each article you chose, answer these questions:

- What method of using words does this article describe? Write these in the circles on the graphic organizer.
- What details about this method are important to know?
- After reading this article, what do you think is the secret to reaching someone with words?

Take notes. Write your answer to the Unit BQ at the bottom of your graphic organizer sheet.

STEP 3: Discuss and Give Reasons

During this step, talk about your answer with your partner.

Discuss your answer to the Unit BQ. Give reasons based on the articles. Think about what information in the articles helped you figure out the secret to reaching someone with words.

Add information to your graphic organizer. In each circle that lists a form of communication, add details about how the form could be the secret to reaching someone with words.

STEP 4: Find and Add Examples

Now, finish your graphic organizer.

Add examples. Brainstorm details from real life and add them to each form of communication on your graphic organizer.

Think about details. Look over all the details about each form of using words. Which details are the most important? Circle them to show that they are the ones that helped you answer the question.

Refine your answer to the Unit BQ. Underline examples that support your answer to the Unit BQ. If you need to, go back and make your answer to the Unit BQ more specific.

STEP 5: Check and Fix

Next, you and your partner will look over your graphic organizers to see whether they could be improved.

Use the rubric. Use the questions on the right side of this page to evaluate your work. Answer each question yes or no. Then trade organizers with your partner. Use the rubric to evaluate your partner's work.

Discuss your evaluations. Explain to your partner why you answered a question yes or no. For every no answer, explain what your partner needs to do to get a yes answer.

Improve your graphic organizer. If your organizer is missing information or information could be improved, make changes.

STEP 6: Practice and Present

Get ready to present your graphic organizer to classmates.

Practice what you want to say. You will use your graphic organizer to explain your answer to the Unit BQ. Think about what you will say. Practice saying it to your partner.

Present your graphic organizer. Explain your answer to the Unit 4 BQ to your classmates. You might want to discuss it with them, or you might want to do a multimedia presentation using an overhead projector, presentation software, or other methods.

RUBRIC

Does the
graphic organizer . . .

- have a detailed answer to the Unit BQ?
- have the titles of at least two articles from Unit 4?
- include details about each method of reaching someone with words?
- give specific examples from articles and real life to explain why one method of reaching someone with words might be the best?

Is it our differences or our similarities that matter most?

These students do not look alike, but they do have things in common. How do you think they are alike? The articles in this unit look at ways that people are alike and ways that they are different. As you read, think about what matters most—our similarities or our differences.

Imagine yourself with a group of your friends. How are you and your friends similar? What makes you uniquely you?

Real-Life Connection

Should some jobs be just for men and other jobs be just for women? Find out what you think. Tell whether you agree or disagree with each statement.

1. Women can be good at fixing cars.
2. Men should not teach grade school.
3. Women do not have what it takes to fly fighter jets.
4. Women do not make good bosses.

Check It Out

Title VII of the Civil Rights Act of 1964 protects the rights of U.S. workers. Under this law, an employer cannot single out and unfairly treat workers because of their race, color, religion, place of birth, or sex. The Equal Pay Act of 1963 forbids an employer from paying workers doing the same job different wages just because of the workers' sex.

WORD BANK

assumption (uh SUHM shuhn) *noun*   When you make an **assumption,** you suppose that something is true without checking to make sure.
EXAMPLE: *My **assumption** that it would not rain was wrong. It stormed all day!*

common (KAH muhn) *adjective*   When something is **common,** it is usual, ordinary, and easy to find.
EXAMPLE: *My illness was not serious. It was just a **common,** everyday cold.*

discriminate (dis KRI muh nayt) *verb*   To **discriminate** against someone is to single the person out and treat the person unfairly.
EXAMPLE: *If you **discriminate** against a classmate, you cannot expect to be treated fairly in return.*

tolerance (TAH luh ruhns) *noun*   **Tolerance** is letting other people have their own beliefs, even if their beliefs differ from yours.
EXAMPLE: *The church, temple, and mosque in our neighborhood show how much **tolerance** we have for different religions.*

Is it our differences or our similarities that matter most?

In the workplace, it is against the law to treat workers differently just because of their sex. However, the law cannot stop people from *thinking* that men and women have different skills and abilities. As you read the article, ask yourself: **Should some jobs be only for men and other jobs only for women?**

Mr. Mom and Madam Speaker

If you were caught in a burning building, would you want a male firefighter to rescue you rather than a female firefighter? If you were sick and in the hospital, would you prefer your nurse to be a man or a woman? The "right" answer would be that it does not matter, but to many people, it matters very much. Whether or not they should, many people secretly **discriminate** against men or women in certain jobs. Many people would rather be rescued by a male firefighter and cared for by a female nurse.

However, more and more people are breaking out of these **common** stereotypes, or molds. It was once unusual for a man to stay home and take care of his children. Child care was considered women's work. Men worked outside the home to support their families. Today, however, about one of every five U.S. dads is the main caregiver.

Women, too, are doing jobs once considered only for the opposite sex. In 2007, a woman became Speaker of the House of Representatives for the first time. Asked about her achievement, Nancy Pelosi said, "Becoming the first woman Speaker will send a message to young girls and women across the country that anything is possible for them." Is it good that women are taking on "men's jobs" and that men are doing "women's work"?

▲ **About one of every ten firefighters is a woman.**

LONG-HELD BELIEFS Some people believe that traditional roles are the best. These people believe that gender stereotypes exist for good reasons. Their main **assumption** is this: Because women have children, they are naturally good at taking care of other people. People with this view also believe that women are good at understanding feelings but bad at understanding "hard" subjects, such as math and science. These people also **assume** that women cannot do hard physical work. Women, they claim, are physically weaker than men and do not make strong leaders.

To these people, men are stronger and more reasonable than women. Because men are more reasonable, these people argue, men can do well in math and science. However, men are not as good as women at taking care of other people.

To support their arguments, people with traditional beliefs point out that many jobs that

> Nine of ten construction workers are men. Almost all day-care workers are women.

were once for men only are still held by men. For example, nine out of ten construction workers are men. More than half of all machine operators, locksmiths, and pest-control workers are men. In addition, most soldiers are men.

Likewise, many jobs traditionally held by women are still **commonly** held by women. In the past, women employed outside the home worked mainly as teachers, nurses, librarians, and office assistants. Today, more than eight of ten people holding these jobs are women. Almost all day-care workers are women, too.

CROSSING OVER On the other hand, many people think that men and women can do any job equally well. They point out that some women are physically strong, while some men are weak. They also note that plenty of women are good at math and science, and plenty of men are good at caregiving. In fact, some male caregivers believe that it is so natural for fathers to care for their children that it is wrong to call them "Mr. Moms." As one male caregiver put it, "It is unfair to 'mom'ify the job. Calling a guy 'Mr. Mom' implies mom *should* be the behind the stroller. That is pretty offensive."

People point to other men and women who have "crossed over" by taking jobs usually done by members of the opposite sex. For example, one man wanted to be a nurse. While in a hospital, he saw nurses caring for newborns. He thought the nurses were lucky to work with babies every day. Then he began to wonder if he could do that job. He took classes, earned a degree, and became a delivery nurse. Now he has his own practice.

Tolerance for crossover workers appears to be growing, though slowly. These workers may be criticized by friends and teased by coworkers, so they have to be strong-willed. They also have to **tolerate** people who are uncomfortable around them.

Though more people are working in jobs outside traditional gender roles, most people still choose traditional jobs. Do they make this decision because some jobs really are right only for men or for women, or do they do so because people have a hard time letting go of long-held beliefs?

It is hard to say. Though sex **discrimination** in the workplace is against the law, attitudes have been slow to change.

WRAP IT UP

Find It on the Page

1. Name a job that was once considered to be for men only.

2. List four jobs that women hold today that they could not have held in the past.

3. Briefly summarize the traditional views about men and women.

Use Clues

4. Why might people find it hard to accept a female firefighter or a male nurse?

5. What advice would you give a female friend who plans to hold a traditionally male job?

6. Would you like to hold a nontraditional job? Explain.

Connect to the Big Question

After reading the article, do you think some jobs should be for men only and other jobs for women only? Why or why not?

Real-Life Connection

How much do you know about work laws for teens? Rate your knowledge on a chart like the one below.

Idea	Know a Lot	Know a Little	Know Nothing
Minimum age teens must be in order to work			
Number of hours teens may work			

Check It Out

The Fair Labor Standards Act lists child labor laws. These laws apply to teen workers across the United States.

- In some states, teens must have permits, or written government permission, in order to work.
- The federal government sets the minimum wage. That is the smallest amount an employer may pay for each hour of work.

WORD BANK

class (klas) *noun*   A **class** is a group of people who are the same in some way, such as in the amount of money they make.
EXAMPLE: *People who work for wages are part of the working **class**.*

identify (y DEN tuh fy) *verb*   When you **identify** something, you tell what it is or who owns it.
EXAMPLE: *I was able to **identify** my math book in the lost-and-found box because I had written my name on the back cover.*

represent (re pri ZENT) *verb*   To **represent** is to stand for someone or something.
EXAMPLE: *Because Danny is the president of the eighth-grade class, he will **represent** all eighth-graders at the board meeting.*

sympathy (SIM puh thee) *noun*   When you have **sympathy** for someone, you understand and share the person's feelings.
EXAMPLE: *The twins feel so much **sympathy** for each other that when one of them cries, the other one cries, too.*

Is it our differences or our similarities that matter most?

A teenager may take your order when you go to a fast-food restaurant to eat. A teen may cook your food, too. Many teens work, doing some of the same kinds of jobs adults do. However, work laws for teens are in some ways different from work laws for adults. As you read the article, ask yourself: Should teen workers be treated differently from adults?

Work Laws for Teens

Teen workers **represent** only a small part of the U.S. workforce. However, even that small part adds up to a big number. More than 6 million American teens work legally. Millions more may work illegally. Teens do many different jobs. For example, they sell clothes, cook hamburgers, and answer phones. There are some jobs that teens are not allowed to do, however. Can you **identify** what these jobs are?

JOBS FOR ADULTS ONLY

Under federal law, you are not allowed to use power-driven machines, such as forklifts and meat slicers, until you are eighteen or older. What's more, you may not do work that requires you to be more than ten feet off the ground. Also, even though the law may allow you to drive at age sixteen, you have to wait until you are eighteen to do a job that requires you to drive.

In addition, laws limit when you may work during the school year and how many hours a day you may work when you have school the next day.

▲ Many teens work to help their families or to earn money to pay for college.

HOURS TEENS MAY WORK			
	Hours a Day	**Hours a Week**	**Working Hours**
Ages 14–15			
School Weeks	3 on school days (8 on Sat.–Sun.)	18	7 A.M. to 7 P.M.
Non-School Weeks	8	40	7 A.M. to 9 P.M.
Ages 16–17			
School Weeks	4 on school days (8 on Fri.–Sun.)	48	7 A.M. to 10 P.M.
Non-School Weeks	8	48	5 A.M. to midnight

Information is from Washington State Department of Labor and Industries, *Teens at Work,* April 2005.

Under federal law, if you are fourteen or fifteen, you may work only three hours a day on school days. You are also limited to a total of eighteen hours a week, and you may not work before 7 A.M. or after 7 P.M. Hours on non-school days and during non-school weeks are different. In most states, you may work longer and later during such periods. (See the table above for standards in one state.)

Are all these rules necessary? Some teens think they are not. These teens say that the government does not have enough **sympathy** for young people who need to work. They argue that teens who have adult responsibilities should be treated like adults at work.

In fact, to get around work laws, some teens **misrepresent** their age. Moreover, some teens who look older than they are sometimes use their appearance to their advantage to get jobs. For these reasons, an employer is required to ask teens to show **identification,** such as a driver's license or birth certificate, to prove how old they are.

REASONS FOR WORK LAWS Why are there so many rules for teen workers? As a **class,** teens are hurt at work almost twice as often as adults. Every year, more than 200,000 fourteen- to seventeen-year-olds are injured, and about seventy teens die from their injuries.

Many people think that teens get hurt so often because teens are not careful. However, experts say it is more often teens' energy and enthusiasm that cause injury. Some teens take on jobs before they have been trained to do them. As a result, they do not know how to avoid injury, and they end up getting hurt.

WHY TEENS WORK In spite of all the rules, many teens work, especially in the summer. In a recent survey, Junior Achievement (JA), a business club for young workers, asked teens why they work. Here are teens' top three reasons.

Extra Cash Some teens want spending money. As a teenager from Virginia explained, "We need stuff like shoes and cell phones, and sometimes our parents don't want to buy us things like that."

Money for School Saving money for college is the second biggest reason teens work. Almost 30 percent of all teens who planned to get summer jobs wanted to save for college.

Life Experience Believe it or not, some teens work just to gain experience. Of course, these teens like paychecks. However, many of them also like learning leadership and teamwork on the job.

Whether or not you choose to work, you should know your rights. Foremost is the right to a safe workplace. Above all, that is what teen work laws are for.

WRAP IT UP

Find It on the Page

1. About how many teenagers in the United States work?

2. List three kinds of jobs that teens are not allowed to do.

3. Briefly summarize the main reasons that teens work.

Use Clues

4. What do you think would happen if there were no work laws for teens?

5. What do you think should be done to cut back on the number of teens hurt on the job?

6. In your opinion, do work laws unfairly limit teens? Explain why or why not.

Connect to the Big Question

After reading the article, do you think teen workers should be treated differently from adult workers? Why or why not?

Real-Life Connection

Reread the title of the article. Then read the article subheadings listed below. What do you think the article will be about? Make a prediction.

- **Genocide in Rwanda**

- **Murekatete Speaks Out**

- **The Killing Continues**

Check It Out

During World War II, Nazi Germany murdered about 6 million Jews. This tragic event is known as the Holocaust (HOH luh kawst). Murdering or seriously harming people because of their race, nationality, culture, or religion is called genocide (JE nuh syd). Recently, genocide has occurred in the African nations of Rwanda and Sudan (in the region of Darfur).

WORD BANK

distinguish (di STING wish) *verb*   To **distinguish** is to tell the difference between similar things.
EXAMPLE: *Though the two guitarists sound almost the same, Ron can **distinguish** them just by listening to them play.*

divide (duh VYD) *verb*   When you **divide** something, you separate it into two or more parts.
EXAMPLE: *Our teacher decided to **divide** our class into four groups.*

generalization (jen ruh luh ZAY shuhn) *noun*   A **generalization** is a statement, rule, or principle that applies to many things.
EXAMPLE: *After my puppy ate part of an old tire, I understood the truth of the **generalization** that dogs will eat almost anything.*

judge (juhj) *verb*   When you **judge** someone or something, you form an opinion about the person or thing.
EXAMPLE: *Dad said he had to listen to both sides of the story before he could **judge** whether my sister or I was right.*

Is it our differences or our similarities that matter most?

Some people who have lived through recent holocausts have told their stories to the world. One such person is Jacqueline Murekatete. As you read the article, ask yourself: How can genocide survivors keep their humanity and dignity?

Holocausts in Rwanda and Darfur

The Rwandan teenager sits quietly in a U.S. TV studio. A news reporter sits across from her, with a list of questions to ask. Terrible memories fill Jacqueline Murekatete's head. She was only nine years old when people killed her family, and it is painful for her to remember the past. On the other hand, she does not want to forget. She wants the world to know what happened in Rwanda.

Murekatete looks at the TV camera and begins her story: "I remember looking up and seeing these men with machetes and clubs," she says. Then she adds, "Just a few hours before, they had probably killed somebody, probably not far from where I was."

What led Rwandans to murder other Rwandans, and why does Murekatete want the world to know what happened in her country?

GENOCIDE IN RWANDA Rwanda is a small country in Central Africa. Two main ethnic groups live there: the Hutu and the Tutsi. These two groups **divide** themselves from each other, even though they have more similarities than they do differences. They speak the same language and share the same traditions.

In 1962, Hutu took over the government. They treated Tutsi with hatred and violence.

▲ Many African children have lost their families in civil wars.

Many Tutsi left the country and started an army called the Rwandan Patriotic Front (FPR). After the FPR invaded Rwanda in 1990, the two groups made peace, but **divisions** remained.

In April, 1994, the Rwandan president, a Hutu, was killed in a plane crash. People claimed the plane had been shot down. Soon, riots broke out. Hutu armed themselves with knives and clubs and began murdering Tutsi. They did not bother to **distinguish** between adults and children.

In July, 1994, the FPR took over Rwanda's capital, and the violence ended. In 100 days, as many as 800,000 people had been murdered. Among them were Murekatete's mother, father, and six brothers and sisters. Murekatete survived because she had been visiting her grandmother in another village when Hutu rioters arrived. Her grandmother later put her in a special home for children without parents, because, in her **judgment,** Murekatete would be safer there. She was right. When Hutu later attacked the grandmother's village, she was murdered.

Jacqueline Murekatete speaks to groups of students about her experiences in Rwanda.

MUREKATETE SPEAKS OUT In October, 1995, Murekatete went to live with an uncle in New York. As the years passed, she wondered if anyone remembered or cared about what had happened in Rwanda. She also wondered if there was anything she could do to keep genocide from happening again. After all, she was just one teenager.

She got her answer during an assembly at her high school in 2002. David Gewirtzman, a Holocaust survivor, came to her school to speak about his experiences. Murekatete was moved by his story. Even though many people might have made the **generalization** that Gewirtzman and Murekatete were very different, she saw many similarities between his story and her own.

After the assembly, she wrote a letter to Gewirtzman. Later, the two teamed up. Since then, they have been traveling together, sharing their experiences with young people. Speaking out has helped Murekatete keep from becoming bitter. She has said, "As a survivor, I felt I have to keep going and have to speak for those people who can no longer speak for themselves, my family included." Her goals are to help other genocide survivors and to prevent future genocides. She wants world leaders to **judge** more quickly if genocide is happening and, if it is, to try to stop it.

THE KILLING CONTINUES Murekatete also speaks about genocide in the Darfur region of Sudan. Since 2003, an armed Arab group called Janjaweed has been starving and murdering non-Arabs there. In addition, Janjaweed has burned villages to the ground, forcing millions of people to leave their homes. The world community has tried to bring peace to Darfur, but the fighting and killing continue.

Darfur's situation reminds Murekatete of Rwanda's. "We have a responsibility to speak out [for] the people who are being killed," she says. "Let us not be silent and indifferent to their suffering."

WRAP IT UP

Find It on the Page

1. Who is Jacqueline Murekatete?

2. What happened to Murekatete in Rwanda?

3. How are the situations in Rwanda and Darfur alike?

Use Clues

4. Why does Murekatete speak out about her experiences in Rwanda?

5. Why do you think Murekatete was so moved by David Gewirtzman's story?

6. What do you think people should learn from Murekatete's experiences?

Connect to the Big Question

After reading the article, how do you think genocide survivors can keep their humanity and dignity?

Real-Life Connection

Many people experience terrible times. Not everyone reacts the same way to them, however. Some people give in to their troubles, but other people overcome them to find happiness. In your opinion, what enables some people to go on when everyone else gives up?

Check It Out

During World War II, the government of Nazi Germany murdered about 6 million Jews. This slaughter is known as the Holocaust (HOH luh kawst). About a sixth of these Jews died in Auschwitz. Auschwitz was a group of camps where the Nazis imprisoned Jews and other people the Nazis considered enemies. Some prisoners were forced to work as slaves. Many died of cold and hunger. Most, however, were murdered by the Nazis.

WORD BANK

probable (PRAH buh buhl) *adjective*   When something is **probable,** it is likely to happen.
  EXAMPLE: *Hector took one look at the dark clouds and said, "It is **probable** that the picnic will be cancelled because of rain."*

separate (SE puh rayt) *verb*   When you **separate** things or people, you keep them apart.
  EXAMPLE: *My teacher decided to **separate** me from Joel because we talked so much in class.*

superficial (soo puhr FI shuhl) *adjective*   When you do things in a **superficial** way, you do them quickly and without much thought.
  EXAMPLE: *Lara's teacher said that she had to research her topic more thoroughly to avoid doing a **superficial** report.*

unify (YOO nuh fy) *verb*   When you **unify** people or things, you bring them together.
  EXAMPLE: *To **unify** us as a team, our coach reminded us that the only way we can win is to work together.*

THE BIG ?

Is it our differences or our similarities that matter most?

A man is torn away from his family. He is stripped of everything he owns. In such a horrible situation, the man could give up on life, but he does not. As you read the article, ask yourself: **How do people overcome suffering by finding meaning in it?**

A Meaningful Life

The guards at Auschwitz were told to **separate** the prisoners into two lines. Viktor Frankl, a Jewish prisoner, did not want to go into the left line. People in that line were murdered right away. Those in the right line were allowed to live for a time so that they could do slave labor. Frankl sneaked into the right line.

Before the Nazis had taken him and his family, Frankl had been writing a book. His wife had helped him hide the papers in the lining of his coat. The papers were lost when Nazis took all his clothes and burned them. Stripped of his belongings, Frankl felt his identity slip away. Somehow, he had to find purpose and meaning in all his suffering in order to survive.

The Nazis forced Jewish people to live in concentration camps.

EARLY INTERESTS Before the war, life had been good to Frankl. As a young student in Vienna, Austria, Frankl had been interested in studying the human mind and behavior. In the late 1920s, when Frankl began his studies, psychology was a fairly new science. After graduation, he became the head doctor in a mental-health clinic.

This map shows where Frankl and his family members were sent.

Unfortunately, as Frankl's career moved forward, so did the Nazis. In 1933, they took over Germany and began to single out Jews there for unfair and increasingly violent treatment. The Nazis wanted to **unify** ethnic Germans across Europe and bring them under Nazi control. When it seemed **probable** that Austria, whose people spoke German, would be taken over by Germany, Frankl grew worried. Austria fell in 1938. Frankl was not arrested right away, however. For a time, he was allowed to stay in Vienna to oversee a Jewish hospital.

CONCENTRATION CAMPS It did not take long for the Nazis to start taking Jews out of Vienna. In 1942, Frankl and his wife, his brother, and his parents were arrested and sent to a holding area for Jews in Theresienstadt. Shortly before this, his sister had moved to Australia.

The Nazis **separated** the members of Frankl's family. Frankl's father stayed in Theresienstadt. There, he died of hunger. Frankl's mother and brother were sent to Auschwitz. They were murdered before the war ended. Frankl's wife died in the Bergen-Belsen concentration camp. During his three years as a prisoner, Frankl lived in several concentration camps, including Auschwitz and Dachau.

CONTROLLING ONE'S ATTITUDE While Frankl was in the camps, he viewed people's behavior from a psychologist's point of view. On tiny pieces of paper, he took notes on what he saw. One of the things he noted was that people reacted very differently to horrible situations. On the surface, people seemed the same, but this view of people, he came to believe, was

probably superficial. There was a clear **separation** between the actions of prisoners who had hope and the actions of those who had given up.

On the other hand, he also saw prisoners reach deep inside themselves to find inner strength. They comforted other people and shared what little food they had. They kept their humanity by looking to the future, planning ways they might **unify** their families again. Equally important, these people stayed true to their values. Though they were surrounded by cruelty, they refused to be cruel. Watching them, Frankl came to believe we can choose what our attitude will be in any situation, no matter how horrible.

Frankl later wrote, "Everything can be taken from a man but one thing: the last of human freedoms—to choose one's attitude in any given set of circumstances, to choose one's own way."

Allied troops freed Frankl and other concentration camp survivors in 1945. After his release, he went on to write more than twenty books. There is meaning in suffering, he said. And meaning is what keeps people alive. Now, more than ten years after Frankl's death, people still find hope and wisdom in his words.

WRAP IT UP

Find It on the Page

1. Who was Victor Frankl?

2. List three things Frankl noted at concentration camps.

3. Briefly summarize what happened to Frankl and his family when the Nazis took over Austria.

Use Clues

4. Why were some prisoners better able to cope with suffering than other prisoners?

5. What do you think people can learn from Frankl?

6. Do you agree that people can choose their attitude in any set of circumstances? Explain.

Connect to the Big Question

After reading the article, how do you think people overcome suffering by finding meaning in it?

PROJECT: Debate

Answer the Big Question: Is it our differences or our similarities that matter most?

You have read articles about similarities and differences. Now, use what you learned to answer the Unit 5 Big Question (BQ).

STEP 1: Form a Group and Choose

Your first step is to pick Unit 5 articles that you like.

Get together. Find a small group to work with.

Read the list of articles. Discuss which articles listed on the left side of this page were the most interesting to you.

Choose two or more articles. Pick articles that you all agree on.

STEP 2: Reread and Answer the Unit Big Question

Your next step is to begin forming your viewpoint for a debate.

Reread the articles you chose. As you reread, think about the Unit BQ.

Answer questions. For each article you chose, answer these questions:

- What issue is this article about?
- How are people in this article alike? How are they different?
- How would you answer the Unit BQ: Is it our differences or our similarities that matter most?

Form teams for the debate. Divide your small group into two opposing teams. One team will present the viewpoint *It is our similarities that matter most.* The other team will present *It is our differences that matter most.*

STEP 3: Find Examples and Discuss Reasons

During this step, begin to develop your argument.

Find examples in the articles. Support your answer to the Unit BQ by listing examples of conflict from the articles you chose. Your examples should clearly support the idea that our similarities matter most or that our differences matter most.

Discuss your reasons. With your team, choose the most convincing reasons to use in the debate and underline them.

STEP 4: Strengthen Your Argument

Now, finish your debate argument.

Choose examples for your argument. Discuss which examples most support your argument. Underline them.

Talk about how to present your argument. To help you, consider these points:

- Think about your audience. Which reasons do you think they will find the most convincing?
- Put your reasons in order. Start with the least convincing and end with the most convincing. Doing this will leave a strong impression.

STEP 5: Strengthen Your Work

Next, you and your team will discuss your debating points to make sure you have a convincing argument.

Use the rubric. Use the questions to evaluate your work. Answer each question yes or no.

Discuss your evaluations. If you have yes answers, can you make those debating points even stronger? If you have any no answers, what can you do to change your argument before you present it?

Improve your argument. Look over your reasons again to make sure that you have chosen convincing ones. Improve your argument before you present it to the class.

STEP 6: Practice and Present

Get ready to debate.

Practice what you want to say. Divide the debating points among your team members. Make sure that you have your reasons in order from least convincing to most convincing. You want to leave a strong impression with your audience.

Present your viewpoint. Present your argument, and the other team will present theirs. You might want to take turns with the other team—with each member of each team presenting a reason and examples to support it. Then have team spokespeople summarize the arguments by repeating all the main points.

Are yesterday's heroes important today?

How does a visit to a museum seem to inspire this teen? This unit explores heroes of the past—from storm chasers and regional heroes to famous athletes and rescue workers. As you read the articles, ask yourself: Are the heroes of yesterday important to us today? If so, in what ways?

Describe a hero from long ago whom you admire. What makes this person from the past someone you can admire in the present?

Real-Life Connection

What do you think this article will be about? Look at the title of the article as well as its subheadings. Write them in a chart like the one below. Write notes about what you can predict about the article after previewing the title and each subheading.

Title	Notes
Subheadings	

Check It Out

Some baseball players have broken rules by "corking" their bats, hoping to hit more homers. Cork is lighter than wood and is springy. Extra springiness means the ball might travel farther. A lighter bat can be swung faster, too.

WORD BANK

accomplishments (uh KAHM plish muhnts) *noun* **Accomplishments** are goals that you meet by working hard.
EXAMPLE: *Randy is proud of his **accomplishments**—getting good grades and being a star baseball player.*

effect (i FEKT) *noun* An **effect** is a result or an influence.
EXAMPLE: *One positive **effect** of studying is better grades.*

emphasize (EM fuh syz) *verb* To **emphasize** something is to stress its importance.
EXAMPLE: *My parents always **emphasize** the benefits of working hard and never giving up.*

occur (uh KUHR) *verb* To **occur** is to happen.
EXAMPLE: *Many special events **occur** during the first week of school.*

Are yesterday's heroes important today?

We are quick to applaud the newest sports star. On the other hand, we may be just as quick to criticize top players when they make mistakes. In fact, yesterday's heroes sometimes become the topic of today's gossip. As you read the article, ask yourself: **Should the passing of time change our views of past heroes?**

Heroes Without Haloes

A dark cloud hangs over several sports heroes. In recent years, reports about dishonest athletes have filled sports columns. The stories in these columns might change our views of certain records and the players who have set them. No sports star is above the rules or the law; but in some cases we should ask ourselves: Is it our heroes who are flawed—or our opinions of them?

THE SOSA SCANDAL During the 2003 baseball season, home-run slugger Sammy Sosa became involved in a scandal. Sosa broke his bat grounding a ball toward second base. When the umpire examined the broken bat, it looked wrong, and for good reason. The bat had been corked. A small piece of cork had been placed inside the bat to make it lighter and easier to swing.

Major League Baseball (MLB) does not allow corked bats. MLB rule 6.06(d) bans using a bat when it "has been altered or tampered with in such a way to improve the distance factor. . . ." The umpire could not let a violation **occur,** so Sosa was thrown out of the game.

▲ Sammy Sosa breaks a bat in 1999, while playing for the Chicago Cubs.

Sosa's career had been filled with **accomplishments:** He had already hit 500 home runs and was seventeenth on MLB's all-time home run list. Sosa was on his way to becoming a legend. When asked about the corked bat, he tried to **emphasize** that he had not intended to use it in the game. "I use that bat for batting practice," he said, "just to put on a show for the fans." He claimed that he grabbed the wrong bat for the game, but many people wonder how he could have made that mistake. Sosa did not want the unfortunate **occurrence** to overshadow what he had already **accomplished.**

▲

Sluggers like Sosa often have favorite bats that they consider to be lucky.

CORKING CONTROVERSY Had Sosa been cheating all along? Were his home run records phony? Many sportswriters and fans thought Sosa had probably used a corked bat in other games. To test that theory, MLB X-rayed all the bats in his locker. The five bats that Sosa had used to **accomplish** milestones—hitting his 500th home run, for example—were also tested. None of the bats contained cork. His penalty of an eight-game suspension was reduced to seven games.

The public wanted to know more about how corked bats perform, so the hosts of a TV show tested the **effect** of a corked bat. They wanted to see whether a ball hit by a corked bat would travel farther. To make sure that the pitches and hits were all the same, the show used machines, rather than people, to throw and hit the ball. The results surprised the hosts and viewers alike.

Balls hit by regulation bats flew at 80 miles per hour, while balls hit by corked bats flew at only 40 miles per hour. Because corked bats have less mass, they absorb some of the force of the hit. Sosa and other hitters who used corked bats had actually lessened their chances of hitting home runs, not increased them!

PUNISH OR PARDON? Should Sosa's name be cleared? Whether or not his use of a corked bat was accidental, it was still illegal. As of early 2008 Sosa was fifth among all-time home run hitters, and his three-time record of hitting sixty or more homers in a season had not yet been broken. Nevertheless, his reputation with baseball fans and sportswriters suffered and may never be the same.

Many other sports heroes have also fallen from grace. Baseball great Pete Rose, who has more career hits (4,256) than any other player, was banned from MLB in 1989 for gambling on his own team, the Cincinnati Reds. Fifteen years later, he admitted he had broken the rules. Because he has apologized, some fans think that he should be allowed into the Baseball Hall of Fame. Rose also hopes to be able to manage a team again someday, but many people still oppose letting Rose back into baseball.

Were Sosa, Rose, and other players who broke the rules treated fairly? Should time clear the names of those who violate sports codes? Despite the mistakes these one-time heroes may have made, their records still stand. However, their place in baseball history is tainted with scandal. No one knows what future fans and sportswriters will think of these "heroes without haloes."

WRAP IT UP

Find It on the Page

1. Who is Sammy Sosa?

2. Why was Sosa thrown out of a game after breaking a bat?

3. Briefly summarize how a TV show tested the effectiveness of corked bats.

Use Clues

4. Why might professional athletes break rules to improve their games?

5. If you were the commissioner of baseball, what would you do to make sure that bats are not corked?

6. How do you feel about athletes who break the rules? Why do you feel this way?

Connect to the Big Question

After reading the article, do you think time changes our views of flawed heroes? Why or why not?

Real-Life Connection

Have you seen people on TV or in the movies jump into their trucks and dash after a storm? Usually, these "storm chasers" are tracking tornadoes. What comes to mind when you think about storm chasers? Jot down your ideas on a word web like the one below. Use the example as a model.

Storm Chasers

fearless

WORD BANK

admirably (AD muh ruh blee) *adverb*   To do something **admirably** is to do it well and in a way that deserves respect.
EXAMPLE: *When Cora was running for class president, she ran her campaign so **admirably** that she won the election.*

influence (IN floo uhns) *verb*   To **influence** people is to have an effect on their actions or thoughts.
EXAMPLE: *My brother knew that if he studied hard, he would **influence** me to become a better student.*

outdated (owt DAY tuhd) *adjective*   When something is **outdated,** it is old-fashioned or no longer in use.
EXAMPLE: *Some adults have **outdated** ideas about what kids find interesting and fun.*

suffering (SUH fuh ring) *noun*   **Suffering** is being in a lot of pain or distress.
EXAMPLE: *The hungry children's **suffering** led us to organize a food drive.*

Are yesterday's heroes important today?

People have always wanted to know what the weather will be, but some people race right into it! Storm chasers follow tornadoes, hurricanes, and other kinds of storms, hoping to see a towering funnel cloud or giant hailstones. As you read the article, ask yourself: Is the work of early storm chasers still important today?

Racing with the Wind

The sky turned a weird green, and black clouds flew in. A severe storm was brewing. Most people stayed indoors, but not Roger Jensen. He hopped into his car and drove directly toward a whirling tornado. He wanted to get the twister on film. One day, his photographs would **influence** weather scientists and pave the way for other storm chasers to come.

Roger Jensen came into the world in 1933. There must have been heavy weather that day in Fargo, North Dakota, because he later said, "I was born loving storms." By the time Jensen was eight years old, storms interested him so much that he stood outside in thunderstorms, smelling the air, feeling the wind, hearing thunder, and watching clouds grow. Soon, Jensen's family moved to a large farm in Minnesota, then to Seattle, Washington. There, Jensen bought his first camera and took pictures of thunderhead clouds over the Cascade Mountains.

▶ **A funnel cloud cuts a path of destruction across the Midwestern countryside.**

THRILL OF THE CHASE When Jensen's family moved back to Fargo, he began chasing storms. During the summer of 1953, he would grab his camera, take the family car, and head toward developing storms. A few years later, he saw his first tornado up close. He was too busy doing farm work to chase the storm, so instead he watched the dark clouds form from the field. Soon, a huge twister struck nearby, tearing apart more than a thousand homes. With wind speeds of up to 300 miles an hour, the tornado was an F-5 on the Fujita scale, a system for measuring a tornado's power.

Jensen's first big chase was in Minnesota in June 1975. He was following a bad storm, but he had not thought that it would turn into a tornado. When it did, the barrel-shaped cyclone moved only six miles in 25 minutes. Jensen easily captured it on film, and the picture made the front page of a weather magazine.

STORM-CHASING EQUIPMENT	
Jensen's Gear	**High-Tech Gear**
Cameras: • Hand-held box camera • 35-mm • Special photo lenses	**Cameras:** • Digital • 35-mm • Tripod • Digital recorder
Weather-monitoring: • Portable radio • *Stormtrack* newsletter	**Weather-monitoring:** • Weather radio • Wireless Internet • Portable radar • Mini TV
Navigation: • Road maps • Weather maps • Compass	**Navigation:** • Maps and atlas • Global Positioning System (GPS)

Information is from *Stormtrack* newsletter and stormtrack.org.

IN PRINT Over the years, Jensen photographed hundreds of storms and cloud formations. His pictures never made him much money, but they were **admirably** exact at capturing aspects of storms that had never before been photographed. Jensen's pictures were so good, in fact, that many of them were printed in newspapers. Other people who gathered facts about weather took notice, and Jensen started to make a name for himself among storm experts. He wrote to famous meteorologists, or people who study the weather. Their national organization printed some of his pictures. So did *Stormtrack*, a newsletter for people interested in storms.

In the 1980s, Jensen developed diabetes, a serious disease. He lost a leg because of the illness and went through great **suffering.** No matter how much he **suffered,** however, he did not let his illness keep him from chasing storms.

TRENDSETTER After he became ill, Jensen moved to a nursing home in "Tornado Alley," a wide strip of country where tornadoes often develop. There, he took pictures of brewing storms.

No one knows who first chased into a storm for adventure, but Jensen was one of the first to take pictures of what he saw. His hobby **influenced** meteorologists. In a now **outdated** approach, they waited for storms to pass, then looked over the damage afterward. Jensen's photos helped them see how storms behave as the storms happen.

Jensen did not have the education, money, or equipment that many storm chasers do now, yet he won **admiration** from many people interested in weather. He was respected by professionals, like Dr. Fujita (of the F-Scale) and David Hoadley, publisher of *Stormtrack*. Jensen's photos also appeared in **influential** books.

Some people complain that hobbyist storm chasers like Jensen get in the way of real research. However, many people believe that Jensen and others like him cleared a path for the scientific research groups that followed.

Jensen died in 2001, at the age of 68. To honor him, a storm chaser summed up Jensen's life in a few words. He wrote that "he was just out there for the love of the storm. . . . Simplicity . . . car, camera, man and storm on the wide open Dakota plains."

WRAP IT UP

Find It on the Page

1. What is a storm chaser?

2. What is the Fujita Scale?

3. Name some of the places where Jensen's photographs were printed.

Use Clues

4. Why do you think Jensen liked taking pictures of storms?

5. What are some ways that storm chasers might help meteorologists?

6. What do you think of people who chase storms? Explain.

Connect to the Big Question

After reading the article, do you think Roger Jensen's work is still important today? Why or why not?

Real-Life Connection

What comes to mind when you think about your heroes? Make a chart like the one below. On the left, list your heroes. On the right, list qualities that make them heroes. Use the examples as a model.

My Heroes	Why They Are My Heroes
my uncle	strong, fearless, kind

bravery (BRAYV ree) *noun* To show **bravery** is to act with courage and without fear.
EXAMPLE: *The firefighters showed great **bravery** when they went into a burning building and rescued a child.*

effect (i FEKT) *noun* An **effect** is a result or an influence.
EXAMPLE: *A sharp headache is a common **effect** of eating ice cream too quickly.*

exaggerate (ig ZA juh rayt) *verb* When you **exaggerate,** you say that something is bigger or more important than it actually is.
EXAMPLE: *Do not **exaggerate** the amount of homework that you have to do.*

overcome (oh vuhr KUHM) *verb* To **overcome** something is to beat it or conquer it.
EXAMPLE: *Aretha had to **overcome** her fear of heights before she could visit the top floor of the building.*

Are yesterday's heroes important today?

Picture Spiderman climbing a skyscraper or Wonder Woman capturing a dangerous criminal. There must be a reason we create heroes like these. As you read the article, ask yourself: How do our heroes reflect who we are?

LARGER THAN LIFE

Doctor Doom has evil plans in mind. He wants to rule the world. There is only one way to stop him—the Fantastic Four! In a flash, the Invisible Woman, the Thing, the Human Torch, and Mister Fantastic spring into action. They use their superhuman powers to fight Doctor Doom. As always, they are able to **overcome** all obstacles. Superheroes always succeed. That is what makes them superheroes.

Like most superheroes, the Fantastic Four are larger than life. They do things ordinary people cannot do, and they use their superpowers to set the world right. We marvel at their amazing feats, and many of us secretly wish that we were like them.

The idea of superheroes is not new. The Fantastic Four are only four examples of American heroes. Long ago, stories were told about people whose **bravery,** strength, and desire to help others made them heroes. Some of these folk heroes were imaginary, like comic-book heroes. Others were legends, or real people whose accomplishments became **exaggerated** over time. In **effect,** they became superheroes.

▲ **Superheroes fill the pages of comic books.**

LOCAL HEROES Folk heroes of the past were often regional, or part of the **culture** of a particular section of the United States. Because different parts of the country had different landscapes and problems, their heroes were different, too. For example, the Midwest and Northwest had thick forests, and many men there worked as lumberjacks, chopping down trees. The lumberjacks created a hero who was like them, only larger than life—a lumberjack phenomenon named Paul Bunyan.

▲ **These statues of Paul Bunyan and Babe the Blue Ox are in Bemidji, Minnesota.**

PAUL BUNYAN Paul Bunyan became a folk hero because of his amazing size and strength. One tall tale says that as a baby he crushed miles of forest when he turned over during a nap. Paul's friend Babe the Blue Ox was equally big and strong—so strong that he could **effectively** pull twists out of crooked roads and straighten them. Paul and Babe were said to have made 10,000 lakes after they walked across Minnesota and their footprints filled with rain. Some folktale experts believe Bunyan was based on a real lumberjack named Bunyon. To this day, many U.S. cities have statues of Paul and Babe.

JOHN HENRY Another folk hero was John Henry. Like Paul Bunyan, Henry was extraordinarily strong and may have been based on a real person. Unlike Bunyan, Henry was a hero from the South.

During the nineteenth century when Henry became famous, railroads were being built across the United States. Legend has it that Henry was the fastest and strongest railroad worker of them all. Freed from slavery after the Civil War, Henry helped lay rail and drill through mountains to build train tunnels.

The nineteenth century was also a time when many new machines were developed. Some people feared that new technology would have negative **effects**, such as the loss of jobs. People did not want machines to replace them. This fear is shown in stories about Henry. He took part in a contest to see if a man could outdrill a machine. Henry won, but the effort killed him. His story has been passed down in a song. One talk-show host recalled, "Ever since I been big enough to remember hearing anybody sing anything at all, I believe I've heard that old song about the strong man that hammered hisself to death on the railroad."

PECOS BILL The Southwest was a rugged land, filled with wild animals, scorching deserts, and tall mountains. Nature sometimes got the best of the cowboys who roamed the land. That may be why they created a hero named Pecos Bill. Tall tales about Pecos Bill describe how he invented things that made cowboys' lives easier—the branding iron to stop cattle-thieving, the lasso to catch stray cattle, and the cowboy lullaby to soothe cattle to sleep. Bill showed his superhuman powers when he rode and tamed tornadoes and roped an entire herd of cattle at one time.

American folk heroes are **brave** and perform great feats. They often reflect and **exaggerate** our **cultural** desires. Whether our heroes fell forests, beat machines, or tame tornadoes, they have qualities we admire.

WRAP IT UP

Find It on the Page

1. What is a superhero?
2. List two folk heroes who have superpowers.
3. Briefly summarize the story of John Henry.

Use Clues

4. What are some reasons that people create superheroes?

5. What do the Fantastic Four have in common with folk heroes of the past?
6. In your opinion, do people need heroes to look up to? Explain why or why not.

Connect to the Big Question

After reading the article, do you think heroes of the past and present reflect who we are? Explain your answer.

Real-Life Connection

How much do you know about Anne Frank and the Holocaust? Rate your knowledge on a chart like the one below.

Idea	Know a Lot	Know a Little	Know Nothing
Anne Frank			
the Holocaust			
Frank's diary			

Check It Out

During World War II, the government of Nazi Germany captured, imprisoned, and murdered Jews throughout Europe. To escape the Nazis, Anne Frank, a young Jewish teenager, went into hiding in Amsterdam with her family. For two years, Anne wrote about her experiences in a diary. Then the family was captured. Anne died in a concentration camp. Her father published her diary after it was found in their hiding place.

WORD BANK

aspects (AS pekts) *noun*   **Aspects** are different sides or parts of a whole.
EXAMPLE: *Anthony is thinking about all **aspects** of getting an after-school job before he makes his decision.*

courage (KUHR ij) *noun*   **Courage** is the mental strength to face a frightening, dangerous, or difficult situation.
EXAMPLE: *It took **courage** for the quarterback to play after the criticism he received from sportswriters.*

endure (in DOOR) *verb*   When you **endure** something, you patiently put up with it, even though you would like to quit.
EXAMPLE: *The track team had to **endure** the hot, sunny weather during practice.*

influence (IN floo uhns) *verb*   To **influence** people is to have an effect on their actions or thoughts.
EXAMPLE: *My grandfather's love of music will continue to **influence** me to practice the guitar.*

Are yesterday's heroes important today?

A group of kids turned to books to pull themselves out of a life of violence and poverty. They read diary entries of students who lived long ago. The entries inspired the kids and allowed them to change their lives. As you read the article, ask yourself: **How can writing from the past influence the present?**

Freedom Writers

For many students, school is not easy. They might have the usual problems that all students have in addition to difficult family situations and personal problems. In their daily lives, these students may have to **endure** fear, violence, and hopelessness. Sometimes, however, students find special meaning in something they study in school. That "something" **influences** them for the better. It helps them find the **courage** to stay in school and graduate.

For one group of kids, inspiration came from a diary written by a girl during World War II. It may seem hard to believe that "tough" kids, some of whom had spent time in a juvenile detention hall, would care about a student from long ago, yet that is what happened at a California high school.

In 1994, a young, **courageous** teacher named Erin Gruwell was assigned to Room 203 in a California high school. The students in 203 had low tests scores and were labeled as unteachable, at-risk, and delinquent. Many of the students were in gangs, and most had never read an entire book. The students came from different countries and cultures. According to one student, they had only three things in common: "We hated school, we hated our teacher, and we hated each other."

▲ Anne Frank enjoyed writing in her diary. In this photo, taken before she and her family were captured, she sits at her desk.

SAD STORIES Life changed for the students in Room 203 after their teacher discovered a racially charged drawing being passed around the room. Gruwell compared the drawing to Nazi hate posters passed around during the Holocaust, when 6 million Jewish people were killed. After Gruwell learned that none of her students had heard of the Holocaust, she introduced the class to *Anne Frank: The Diary of a Young Girl.* Anne's story was filled with meaning for the students. Like Anne, they had **endured** fear, violence, and prejudice.

> As they began to find their inner voices, the students found power in writing.

The students also read *Zlata's Diary: A Child's Life in Sarajevo.* Zlata, a normal eleven-year-old girl living in Sarajevo (now in Bosnia and Herzegovina), wrote about clothes, music, and boys. However, in 1991 her diary entries changed. Bombs began falling in her town, and violence, starvation, and fear became part of her daily life.

The students in Room 203 were shocked to learn how much they had in common with these two girls. The girls' diary entries described violence, yet their writing was also filled with great hope. The students learned a valuable lesson from these diaries: the importance of tolerance. If the students could relate to Anne and Zlata, the students might be able to relate to one another.

IN THEIR OWN WORDS The students in Room 203 began writing about **aspects** of their own lives. They wrote stories, poems, and rap songs about their daily struggles. The writing was about difficult issues on the students' minds: gang violence, racism, immigration, prejudice, and fear. However, the students also wrote about their desire to find a place in the world and about their dreams for the future.

As they began to find their inner voices, the students found power in writing. They decided to call themselves the Freedom Writers, in honor of the Freedom Riders who challenged racism during the 1960s. Outside of Room 203, the Freedom Writers were alone, but in their classroom, they were a team. They shared stories of pain and **courage.** They cried and laughed with each other.

The most important discovery the Freedom Writers made was that their lives mattered. They could be **influential,** and their **influence** could change their own lives and the lives of others for the better.

The students had another story to tell when Miep Gies visited them in Long Beach. She helped hide the Frank family from the Nazis during World War II. The class also spent five days with Zlata, exchanging stories and sharing their writing. The students realized they could change their lives through writing, and they did. All one-hundred and fifty Freedom Writers graduated from high school— something that no one thought they would do. Many even went on to college and earned degrees.

Perhaps, however, the Freedom Writers' most surprising achievement was a book. The students who once had never read a book ended up writing one when their diary entries were published in *The Freedom Writers Diary.*

WRAP IT UP

Find It on the Page

1. Who were the Freedom Writers?

2. After whom did the Freedom Writers name themselves?

3. What two books inspired the Freedom Writers?

Use Clues

4. What effect did writing their own stories have on the students in Room 203?

5. How do you think the students' book of personal stories can help other students?

6. In your opinion, is it easier to write about difficult experiences than to talk about them? Explain.

Connect to the Big Question

After reading the article, do you think writing from the past can influence the present? Explain why or why not.

Real-Life Connection

Suppose you received twenty dollars as a gift. What would you do with the money? Would you save it or spend it? Would you consider giving the money to a stranger in need? Would you be willing to hand over your money to a family member in need? Jot down what you would do and why.

Check It Out

Philanthropy (fuh LAN thruh pee) is the act of giving money or time to help others in need. Many organizations organize volunteer efforts—the American Red Cross, AmeriCorps, and the United Way are a few examples.

WORD BANK

accomplishments (uh KAHM plish muhnts) *noun*   **Accomplishments** are goals that you meet by working hard.
EXAMPLE: *Shanise made a list of her accomplishments to show what she learned in her classes.*

effect (i FEKT) *noun*   An **effect** is a result or an influence.
EXAMPLE: *A stuffy nose is a common effect of having a cold.*

endure (in DOOR) *verb*   When you **endure** something, you patiently put up with it, even though you would like to quit.
EXAMPLE: *I do not know if I can endure another minute of listening to my little brother practice his trombone.*

exaggerate (ig ZA juh rayt) *verb*   When you **exaggerate,** you say that something is bigger or more important than it actually is.
EXAMPLE: *That runner is fast, but you exaggerate if you say he is the fastest runner in the world.*

overcome (oh vuhr KUHM) *verb*   To **overcome** something is to beat it or conquer it.
EXAMPLE: *I am determined to finish school, and I will overcome any obstacle that gets in my way.*

THE BIG ?

Are yesterday's heroes important today?

When an earthquake caused a deadly tsunami in Indonesia in 2004, Americans donated millions of dollars to help people they had never met. Eight months later, Americans were called on to help again when a hurricane struck the United States. As you read the article, ask yourself: **How do natural disasters change people?**

The Kindness of Strangers

Children thought of creative ways to help raise money for Katrina victims.
▼

During the summer of 2005, TV viewers watched closely as a strong hurricane developed in the Gulf of Mexico. Within days, Hurricane Katrina grew into a deadly storm. The view from above the hurricane showed a monstrous storm covering the entire Gulf of Mexico. People who lived on the Gulf Coast hoped that the storm would lose its power before it hit, but their hopes were not realized.

On August 29, 2005, Hurricane Katrina reached land. According to the National Hurricane Center, Katrina was a Category 4 hurricane. Packing winds of 125 to 140 miles per hour, the storm hit the southern Louisiana coast. The winds had a terrible **effect.** They turned thousands of homes into piles of sticks. Communities along the Gulf were wiped out. Then the ocean took its turn, and a wall of water pounded the levees that protected the city of New Orleans. When these artificial banks collapsed, water poured in, and most of the city and surrounding towns were left under water.

Unit 6 **185**

Pictures of the storm's terrible **effects** filled TV screens and newspapers. Photographs showed people and animals stranded on rooftops. Buildings were flattened, roads were washed away, and people were in shock. Though help was, at first, slow to get to flooded areas, it was not slow to reach charities like the Red Cross.

VOLUNTEERS AND DONATIONS Americans can be generous. When people are in need, some Americans willingly open up their wallets and give. Mother nature may have created a disaster, but human nature answered it with an outpouring of gifts. There is no need to **exaggerate** the reports of generosity—the donations of money, food, clothing, and time from people all over the country were astonishing.

A family from Baton Rouge, Louisiana, was like many families all over the United States. The members of the family did not know anyone who was affected by Katrina, but that did not stop them from helping. Family members loaded up their car with baby food, clothes, sheets, and shoes, then unloaded the gifts at a donation center.

The number of people who offered to help the Red Cross was touching. In fact, so many new volunteers offered their help that the group set up one-day training classes. The volunteers included doctors, teachers, construction workers, farmers, and many others. (See the table for more information about how the Red Cross helped after Hurricane Katrina hit.)

One man promised to give five days of work. When he got to the disaster scene, he saw that not much

RED CROSS RESPONSE TO HURRICANE KATRINA	
Volunteers	244,000
Red Cross Shelters	1,400
Overnight stays	3.8 million
Meals served	68 million
People helped	1.4 million

Information is from RedCross.com.

could be **accomplished** in five hundred days, much less five. Still, he was determined to **overcome** the obstacles, so he rolled up his sleeves and began to work. He found many homes filled with water, mud, mold, and garbage. To clean up the mess, he and others used sledgehammers and shovels. They filled wheelbarrows with ruined possessions and pulled down rotting walls. It was tough work, but the volunteers kept at it. If the victims could **endure** the terrible **effects** of the hurricane, the volunteers felt that they should show **endurance**, too.

LEMONADE, HAIRCUTS, AND TOYS In addition to helping clean up and rebuild, volunteers also did creative things to raise money for the relief effort. In one small town, a pair of young children set up a lemonade stand. One kind person donated $100! In three days, the children raised $2,300 for Katrina's victims.

In California, a hairstylist came up with a different idea. She gave free haircuts as donations to the United Way. School groups and Cub Scouts started their own relief efforts. They stuffed backpacks with clothes and toys for children. These are just a few examples of the extraordinary **accomplishments** of ordinary, compassionate people.

What kept everyone going? The smile of someone who has just received help can be a great motivator. A tired volunteer covered in mud told reporters that a smile like this "turns you around to swing the sledge [hammer] for one more hour." It is a smile that means that hope is not lost and that **overcoming** disaster is not impossible.

WRAP IT UP

Find It on the Page

1. When did Hurricane Katrina reach land?

2. List three effects of Hurricane Katrina.

3. Briefly summarize how the Red Cross helped Katrina victims.

Use Clues

4. Why do you think the volunteers were willing to help strangers?

5. What lessons do you think we can learn from Katrina?

6. Some people think that disasters like Katrina bring out the best in people. Do you agree? Explain.

Connect to the Big Question

After reading the article, how do you think natural disasters change people? Explain.

Real-Life Connection

How much do you know about World War II? Rate your knowledge on a chart like the one below.

Idea	Know a Lot	Know a Little	Know Nothing
Who was involved in the war			
Where the island of Iwo Jima is located			
Why the battle of Iwo Jima was important			

Check It Out

To raise money to pay for World War II, the government sold war bonds. These bonds were loans to the government. Times were hard for many Americans, so the government had to persuade people to buy bonds. Ads for bonds featured war heroes, movie stars, and famous athletes.

 **WORD BANK**

courage (KUHR ij) *noun*   **Courage** is the mental strength to face a frightening, dangerous, or difficult situation.
EXAMPLE: *Omar showed a lot of **courage** when he dived into the cold water to save the little boy.*

imitate (I muh tayt) *verb*   When you **imitate** someone or something, you try to be like the person or thing.
EXAMPLE: *My little brother likes to **imitate** the singers on TV, so he sings and dances around the living room.*

suffering (SUH fuh ring) *noun*   **Suffering** is being in a lot of pain or distress.
EXAMPLE: *The stray dog's **suffering** was obvious, so we took him in and gave him food and shelter.*

symbolize (SIM buh lyz) *verb*   When things represent or stand for something else, they **symbolize** it.
EXAMPLE: *Did you know that yellow roses **symbolize** friendship?*

Are yesterday's heroes important today?

Movies often portray Native Americans as warriors. In reality, Native Americans have often been warriors for the United States. Native Americans served in both world wars and during conflicts in Korea, Vietnam, Iraq, and Afghanistan. Some, like Ira Hayes, even became heroes. As you read the article, ask yourself: **What can we learn from Ira Hayes?**

HONORABLE WARRIORS

On February 19, 1945, U.S. Marines landed on Iwo Jima, a tiny island in the South Pacific Ocean. The island was very important to the United States and its allies. It had airfields used by enemy fighter planes from Japan. If the island was captured, American fighter planes could use the airfields to fly to Japan. The Japanese knew the strategic value of the island, and they had no intention of giving it up without a **courageous** fight.

The battle at Iwo Jima was a hard victory for the United States. The Marines lost more than 6,000 men. One of the main goals of the battle was to take control of Mount Suribachi, a non-active volcano that is the highest point on the island. It gives the best view of all the beaches. On February 23, four days after the battle began, the Marines reached their goal.

THE PHOTOGRAPH When six Marines raised an American flag on Iwo Jima, a photographer happened to be there. The photograph was published in several U.S. newspapers. It came to **symbolize** American victory and fighting spirit.

This image of U.S. soldiers raising the flag ▶ at Iwo Jima inspired many Americans.

(Showing that life can **imitate** art, New York firefighters raised an American flag on September 11, 2001, to memorialize the very different fight at the World Trade Center.) None of the Marines was hurt during the flag raising, but three of the six men pictured in the photograph later died in combat on Iwo Jima.

The famous photograph raised American spirits at a time when Americans were losing faith in winning the war. The photograph was more influential than the men in the photo could have ever dreamed. John Bradley, Rene Gagnon, and Ira Hayes, the three men pictured who survived Iwo Jima, became instant heroes. They were called home and attended parades in cities all over the country. They went to banquets, gave interviews, and helped sell war bonds. The bonds helped pay for food, clothes, and shelter for American soldiers. Hayes wanted to return to the front lines, where he could show his **courage** and be a real warrior, rather than a **symbolic** one. However, his wish did not come true.

> During a Pima ceremony, the Pima chief told Hayes to be an honorable warrior.

HAYES'S HISTORY Hayes, a Pima Indian, was born on January 12, 1923, in Sacaton, Arizona. The Pimas lived on the Gila River Indian Reservation, desert land with little water for farming. When Hayes was born, Native Americans did not have rights as American citizens, and Arizona had been a state for only eleven years. However, by the time World War II began, the situation had changed. Native Americans had been given citizenship in 1924, and more than 40,000 Native Americans had **courageously** served the United States during World War II. Hayes was one of them. He joined the Marine Corps just months after the bombing of Pearl Harbor. During a Pima ceremony before he left, the Pima chief told Hayes to be an honorable warrior.

Hayes took courses with the U.S. Marine Corps Parachutist School and was admired by his peers. Within a few years, he was ordered overseas to take part in the invasion of Iwo Jima. Hayes had no way of knowing a photograph would make him a hero.

AMERICAN HEROES It was President Franklin D. Roosevelt who called on Hayes and his fellow flag raisers to join the war bond drive. Hayes disliked the bond-selling trips because he did not think of himself as a hero. He said that the real heroes were his "good buddies" who had died on Iwo Jima.

Later, President Truman also called Hayes an American hero. However, Hayes still did not see himself in that light. He said, "How could I feel like a hero when only five men in my platoon of forty-five survived, when only twenty-seven men in my company of two-hundred and fifty managed to escape death or injury?" Hayes believed that there was nothing **courageous** about what he did on February 23, 1945. In fact, Hayes said that there were times when he wished the photograph had never been taken.

Unfortunately, Hayes did not cope well with fame. The publicity took a toll on him, and his **suffering** led to his ruin. Hayes died on the reservation as a result of exposure to bad weather. At his death, he was only thirty-two years old. He was buried at the Arlington Cemetery with full military honors.

WRAP IT UP

Find It on the Page

1. Who was Ira Hayes?

2. Why was the island of Iwo Jima important to the war effort?

3. Briefly summarize how the famous photograph on Iwo Jima came to be taken.

Use Clues

4. Why do you think the photograph meant so much to Americans?

5. What connections can you find between the battle at Iwo Jima and the "battle" at the World Trade Center?

6. In your opinion, was Hayes correct when he said that the real heroes were the men who had died? Explain.

Connect to the Big Question

After reading the article, what do you think we can learn from Ira Hayes? Explain.

Real-Life Connection

What do you know about the civil rights movement in the United States? Answer these true-false questions to find out.

1. Racial segregation is the separation of people by race.
2. Protests against racial segregation started in the 1970s.
3. Medgar Evers was a civil rights leader before Dr. King.
4. Evers was the first African American to attend a white school.

Check It Out

In the past, sections of the United States were racially segregated. "Blacks" could not drink at "white" water fountains, eat at "white" lunch counters, or go to "white" schools. Tired of being treated like second-class citizens, African Americans of the 1950s began to protest against discrimination.

aspects (AS pekts) *noun*   Aspects are different sides or parts of a whole.
EXAMPLE: *Maybe you should think about the different **aspects** of the problem before you try to find a solution.*

bravery (BRAYV ree) *noun*   To show **bravery** is to act with courage and without fear.
EXAMPLE: *Mo's **bravery** showed when she stood up to the bully.*

emphasize (EM fuh syz) *verb*   To **emphasize** something is to stress its importance.
EXAMPLE: *Our teacher liked to **emphasize** being on time.*

literal (LI tuh ruhl) *adjective*   Things that are **literal** stick to the facts or follow the exact meaning of words.
EXAMPLE: *When I say, "Hit the road," I do not mean it in the **literal** sense—I mean that you should leave.*

symbolize (SIM buh lyz) *verb*   When things represent or stand for something else, they **symbolize** it.
EXAMPLE: *Flags **symbolize** the countries they come from.*

Are yesterday's heroes important today?

Nearly fifty years have passed since the Civil Rights Act became law. Are there still wrongs that need to be righted? As you read the article, ask yourself: Why do certain leaders from the past still inspire and challenge us?

LONG ROAD TO JUSTICE

Before the Civil Rights Act of 1964, African Americans did not have the same rights and privileges as whites. Older laws allowed schools to be segregated. Public places, such as restaurants, movie theaters, and restrooms, were sometimes segregated.

For many of today's young people, well-known heroes like Dr. Martin Luther King, Jr., and Rosa Parks **symbolize bravery** and the civil rights movement. Fewer young people know the name Medgar Evers, even though he helped paved the way for other civil rights leaders and for the Civil Rights Act.

Evers was born in Decatur, Mississippi, in 1925. As a young man, he joined the army and served in World War II. Afterward, he went to Alcorn College in Mississippi, where he studied business. His first job was as a traveling insurance salesman.

EVERS ORGANIZES In Mississippi, African Americans were often mistreated. Evers had known racism since he was a child. During his travels around the state as a salesman, Evers became frustrated with the conditions in which many African Americans had to live.

▲ This picture of a "whites-only" sign was taken in Mississippi in 1961.

He knew that the lives of African Americans would never improve if they did not **bravely** take a stand.

There were many **aspects** to Evers's fight against racism. Evers joined the National Association for the Advancement of Colored People (NAACP) and applied to law school at the University of Mississippi. Even though the Supreme Court had ruled against segregation in schools, he was not allowed to attend the school because of his race.

In 1954, Evers became Mississippi's first field secretary for the NAACP. As secretary, he spoke out against segregation.

This student sit-in took place in 1965 in Jackson, Mississippi.

A supporter of peaceful protest, Evers would **emphasize** the importance of using nonviolent methods to gain equality. He organized sit-ins, or demonstrations in which protestors sat on the ground to block entrances to public places. Evers also organized voter-registration drives and urged people to vote.

THREATS BECOME REAL Evers spent hours away from his family while he was organizing demonstrations, marches, picket lines, and boycotts. As a result of his efforts, angry whites threatened his life. Still, Evers did not waver in his decision to protest. He was determined to push for equal rights, no matter what.

Then the threats became real. In May 1963, Evers's home in Jackson, Mississippi, was firebombed. Luckily, no one was hurt. Sadly, however, the following month brought a successful attempt on Evers's life. On June 12, as Evers walked from his car to his house, he was shot in the back. He died at the hospital within an hour.

The African American community did not react with fear. Instead, his death became a **symbol** of the need for justice. Protestors knew that fear was not an option. The situation called for **bravery.** They found their courage and continued Evers's work.

JUSTICE IS DELAYED The gun used to kill Evers was found near his body. The fingerprints were still fresh. Police arrested Byron De La Beckwith for Evers's murder. After two trials, Beckwith was released because the all-white jury could not agree on a verdict.

In 1989, however, the case was reopened because of new information about how jury members were chosen and because of new evidence. Though many people in Mississippi did not want to try Beckwith a third time, he went to trial again in 1994. Finally, with a jury made up of black people as well as white people, Beckwith was found guilty of murder and sentenced to life in prison. It had taken thirty-one years for the killer to be brought to justice.

Evers once said, "You can kill a man, but you can't kill an idea." The **literal** meaning of his words has been proven true, because his legacy lives on. His family continued the fight for civil rights. His brother Charles took Evers's position at the NAACP, and in 1969 Charles became the first African American mayor in Mississippi. Evers's wife, Myrlie, became chairperson of the board of directors for the NAACP. In addition, the Medgar Evers Institute in Jackson, Mississippi, and Medgar Evers College in New York City serve students of all backgrounds. Evers would have been proud.

WRAP IT UP

Find It on the Page

1. Who was Medgar Evers?

2. Why did Evers have to give up his dream of attending law school?

3. List three ways that Evers fought racism.

Use Clues

4. Why do you think it took so long for Evers's murderer to be convicted?

5. What can we learn from people like Medgar Evers?

6. Do you think that Evers should have risked his and his family's lives the way he did? Explain.

Connect to the Big Question

After reading the article, why do you think figures from the past continue to inspire us today?

Real-Life Connection

What do you think this article will be about? Look at the title of the article as well as its subheadings. Write them in a chart like the one below. Write notes about what you can predict about the article after previewing the title and each subheading.

Title	Notes
Subheadings	

Check It Out

September 11, 2001, is a date that many Americans will remember as long as they live. On that date, terrorists attacked New York City and Washington, D.C. They hijacked several planes. Two planes crashed into the World Trade Center, one crashed into the Pentagon, and a fourth crashed into a field in the Pennsylvania countryside.

admirably (AD muh ruh blee) *adverb*   To do something **admirably** is to do it well and in a way that deserves respect.
  EXAMPLE: *Lisa performed **admirably** when she sang a solo.*

imitate (I muh tayt) *verb*   When you **imitate** someone or something, you try to be like the person or thing.
  EXAMPLE: *Our cat tries to **imitate** our dog by playing fetch.*

observe (uhb ZUHRV) *verb*   To **observe** is to look at something carefully or to study it.
  EXAMPLE: *Our science teacher wanted us to **observe** the changes in certain plants over a two-month period.*

outdated (owt DAY tuhd) *adjective*   When something is **outdated,** it is old-fashioned or no longer in use.
  EXAMPLE: *While looking at the 2000 yearbook, we noticed that the clothes people wore already look **outdated**.*

Are yesterday's heroes important today?

The terrorist attacks on September 11, 2001, touched people across the United States and around the world. Firefighters, police officers, paramedics, veterinarians, and volunteers all came to help rescue workers search in the rubble. As you read the article, ask yourself: **What makes people help each other in times of crisis?**

Heroes of 9/11

On the morning of September 11, 2001, the skies over New York City were blue and clear. Most New Yorkers were beginning their workday. Other Americans were waking up and watching the news on TV. No one was prepared for what happened next. At about 8:45 A.M., a plane crashed into Tower One of the World Trade Center. Within a few minutes, another plane hit Tower Two. The buildings burned ferociously, then collapsed. At about 9:40 A.M., a third plane crashed into the Pentagon. Soon after, a plane on its way to Washington, D.C., crashed in a Pennsylvania field. By that time, it was clear that the United States was under attack.

At first, Americans were in shock. People stayed glued to their TV sets, trying to **observe** the events and make sense of what had happened. Though frightened and angry, they knew it was a time to come together and help one another.

Firefighters were among the heroes of 9/11. ▶

NEW YORK CITY FIRE DEPARTMENT The most courageous citizens in the immediate aftermath of the attacks were New York City firefighters and rescue workers. They rushed into the World Trade Center Towers without hesitation. One off-duty female firefighter knew the city would need all the help it could get, but getting to the scene was not easy. Traffic was at a standstill, so she ran to the Twin Towers.

> **Most of the digging was done by hand as rescue teams desperately searched for survivors.**

Fire crews were trying to hook up water supplies to fight smaller fires because hydrants had been crushed by the buildings' collapse. Firefighters walked in ankle-deep dust, searching for survivors. One firefighter described his grim **observations** this way: "It's a site where guys have broken their legs, where people have cut themselves open on the metal, where you are breathing in dust and smoke."

Working at the site was very difficult for emergency responders because of the huge piles of rubble. Cranes and other heavy equipment were brought to the scene, but most of the digging was done by hand as rescue teams desperately searched for survivors. So many people wanted to help that volunteers arrived from both nearby neighborhoods and faraway states to offer their assistance. The New York City firehouses were full and busy.

SEARCH AND RESCUE DOGS Firefighters were not the only rescuers. More than 300 canine rescue teams joined firefighters and police officers to look for survivors. Like their human leaders, the dogs worked **admirably.** They searched in dangerous dark spaces and crawled on their bellies through the ruins.

Rescue dogs are driven to succeed. They will search for a scent without a break. However, even the dogs looked frustrated and hopeless when they could not find survivors. The dogs were tired, suffered injuries, and became depressed. Their handlers had to **imitate** successful rescues so that the dogs would feel well again. At the same time, the dogs lifted the spirits of rescue workers. Experts have long **observed** that dogs can help reduce people's stress. The dogs offered emotional relief to rescue workers.

KIND NEIGHBOR While rescue workers tried to locate survivors and help the injured, private citizens did what they could to help. One man, named John, invited people into his tiny apartment to use the phone. People wanted to call their loved ones to let them know they were safe. However, cell phone service was poor, and **outdated** pay phones had long lines of people waiting to use them.

One person who was anxious about entering John's apartment said that it was not safe to go into a stranger's home in New York City. Once inside the apartment, however, the stranger drank a glass of water and felt the kindness in the room. The man had just escaped from the ground floor of the World Trade Center.

John opened up his home to help those who needed a safe place to recover for a few minutes. Helping others also helped him. He had seen the first plane sticking out of the north tower. The strangers in his home helped him think about the present rather than the horrible events he had witnessed. Later, his relatives helped him pay his huge phone bill because they **admired** what he did. He was one of many heroes in New York City; Washington, D.C.; and Pennsylvania that day. In the sad days that followed, many more Americans donated their time and their money to help clean up and to heal the country.

WRAP IT UP

Find It on the Page

1. What happened on September 11, 2001?

2. What kinds of difficulties did New York City firefighters face on September 11?

3. Briefly summarize how rescue dogs helped after the attacks.

Use Clues

4. What did this tragedy reveal about people in New York City?

5. What did the firefighters, rescue dogs, and John have in common?

6. Why do you think people showed such courage rather than despair?

Connect to the Big Question

After reading the article, why do you think people help each other in times of crisis?

PROJECT: Poster

Answer the Big Question: Are yesterday's heroes important today?

You have read about heroes from the past and present. Now, use what you learned to answer the Unit 6 Big Question (BQ).

UNIT 6 ARTICLES

Heroes Without Haloes,
pp. 168–171

Racing with the Wind,
pp. 172–175

Larger Than Life,
pp. 176–179

Freedom Writers,
pp. 180–183

The Kindness of Strangers,
pp. 184–187

Honorable Warriors,
pp. 188–191

Long Road to Justice,
pp. 192–195

Heroes of 9/11,
pp. 196–199

STEP 1: Partner Up and Choose

Your first step is to pick Unit 6 articles that you like.

Get together. Find a partner to work with.

Read the list of articles. Discuss which articles listed on the left side of this page were the most interesting to you.

Choose two or more articles. Pick articles that you both agree on.

STEP 2: Reread and Answer the Unit Big Question

Your next step is to answer the Unit BQ with your partner.

Reread the articles you chose. As you read, think about what the Unit BQ means.

Answer questions. For each article you chose, answer these questions:

- Who is this article about?
- What makes a person a hero?
- Was this person a hero in the past? Is this person still a hero?

Answer the Unit BQ. Answer the Unit BQ on the basis of the people you read about. Do you think that people who were heroes in the past are still heroes?

STEP 3: Discuss and Give Reasons

During this step, talk about your answer and start your poster.

Discuss your answer to the Unit BQ. Think about the people in the articles and whether their heroic actions of the past make them heroes today. What images or words could you add to a visual display about the Unit BQ?

Start collecting items for your poster. You might want to write quotations from the articles and collect pictures from Web sites and print materials. You might also want to write words that tell what makes these people heroes.

STEP 4: Find and Add More Examples

Now, finish your poster.

Think more deeply about the Unit BQ. Discuss with your partner other heroes that might help you answer the Unit BQ. These heroes might be from fiction or from real life.

Add examples to the poster. Include pictures, written descriptions, or quotations that explain your answer to the Unit BQ. Choose examples that will support your answer and will interest viewers.

STEP 5: Check Your Work

Next, you and your partner will look over your poster to see if you can improve it.

Use the rubric. Use the questions on the right to evaluate your work. Answer each question yes or no.

Discuss your evaluations. Use the rubric answers as a guide to improve your work. You might want to rearrange items on the poster, add color, add more specific ideas, and so on.

Finish the poster. Use ideas from your evaluation discussion to finish your poster. If time and resources allow, you might want to create a multimedia presentation to showcase images and sounds that relate to your answer to the Unit BQ.

STEP 6: Practice and Present

Get ready to present your poster to classmates.

Practice what you want to say. You will use ideas reflected on the poster to explain your answer to the Unit BQ. Think about what you will say. Each of you might want to do one part of the presentation. Practice together.

Present your poster. Tell your answer to the Unit 6 BQ to your classmates. Explain clearly how the items on the poster answer the question. If you chose to do a multimedia presentation, introduce your answer before showing your work to classmates. Be prepared to answer their questions.

> ## RUBRIC
>
> **Does the poster . . .**
> - clearly show the answer to the Unit BQ?
> - have words or images that relate to ideas in the articles?
> - have an appearance—including color, layout, and number of images chosen—that will interest viewers?

GLOSSARY

This glossary will help you quickly find definitions of Word Bank words.

A

accomplishments (uh KAHM plish muhnts) *noun*   **Accomplishments** are goals that you meet by working hard.

accumulate (uh KYOO myuh layt) *verb* When you **accumulate** something, you gather or collect it little by little.

admirably (AD muh ruh blee) *adverb* To do something **admirably** is to do it well and in a way that deserves respect.

analyze (A nuh lyz) *verb*   When you **analyze** something, you study its parts and see how they fit together.

argument (AHR gyuh muhnt) *noun*   An **argument** is a reason or set of reasons for or against a point of view.

arrange (uh RAYNJ) *verb*   When you **arrange** something, you put it in order or prepare for it.

aspects (AS pekts) *noun*   **Aspects** are different sides or parts of a whole.

assumption (uh SUHM shuhn) *noun*   When you make an **assumption**, you suppose that something is true without checking to make sure.

B

benefit (BE nuh fit) *noun*   A **benefit** is something good that results from an action.

bias (BY uhs) *noun*   To have a **bias** means to prefer or reject one group or one thing over another every time.

bravery (BRAYV ree) *noun*   To show **bravery** is to act with courage and without fear.

C

cause (kawz) *verb*   To **cause** something to happen is to be the reason that it happens.

challenge (CHA luhnj) *verb*   When you **challenge** someone's statements or decisions, you say the person is or might be wrong.

class (klas) *noun*   A **class** is a group of people who are the same in some way, such as in the amount of money they make.

common (KAH muhn) *adjective* When something is **common**, it is usual, ordinary, and easy to find.

compromise (KAHM pruh myz) *noun*
When you reach a **compromise** with
someone else, you both give up
something you want in order to settle
an argument.

confirm (kuhn FUHRM) *verb*   To **confirm** something is to agree with it or
demonstrate that it is true.

connection (kuh NEK shuhn) *noun*
A **connection** is a link or similarity
between people or things.

consider (kuhn SI duhr) *verb*   When
you **consider** something, you think
about it carefully.

contradict (kahn truh DIKT) *verb*
When you **contradict** someone, you
argue against what he or she says.

control (kuhn TROHL) *verb*   When
you **control** something, you guide it
or rule over it.

courage (KUHR ij) *noun*   **Courage** is
the mental strength to face a frightening, dangerous, or difficult situation.

criteria (kry TIR ee uh) *noun*   **Criteria**
are standards or tests that you can
use to judge something.

cultural (KUHLCH ruhl) *adjective*
Something that is **cultural** has to do
with a particular group's beliefs, values, and customs.

D

decision (di SI zhuhn) *noun*   When
you make a **decision,** you choose one
thing or course of action over another.

derive (di RYV) *verb*   To **derive** is to
get something from another source.

detail (di TAYL) *noun*   A **detail** is a
small part of something bigger.

detect (di TEKT) *verb*   When you **detect**
something, you notice its existence.

development (di VE luhp muhnt)
noun   When something undergoes
development, it becomes bigger,
fuller, or better.

discriminate (dis KRI muh nayt)
verb   To **discriminate** against someone is to single the person out and
treat the person unfairly.

discrimination (dis kri muh NAY
shuhn) *noun*   **Discrimination** is
treating people unfairly because they
belong to a particular group.

distinguish (di STING wish) *verb*   To
distinguish is to tell the difference
between similar things.

divide (duh VYD) *verb*   When you
divide something, you separate it into
two or more parts.

doubtful (DOWT fuhl) *adjective*
Something is **doubtful** when you are
uncertain that it is true.

E

effect (i FEKT) *noun*   An **effect** is a result or an influence.

emphasize (EM fuh syz) *verb*   To **emphasize** something is to stress its importance.

endure (in DOOR) *verb*   When you **endure** something, you patiently put up with it, even though you would like to quit.

equal (EE kwuhl) *adjective*   Things that are **equal** are the same or fairly balanced.

essential (i SEN shuhl) *adjective*   When something is **essential**, it is necessary and important.

evidence (E vuh duhns) *noun*   **Evidence** is proof that something is true, or it is knowledge you use to back up an argument.

exaggerate (ig ZA juh rayt) *verb*   When you **exaggerate**, you say that something is bigger or more important than it actually is.

explanation (ek spluh NAY shuhn) *noun*   When you give an **explanation** of something, you give details or reasons that help other people understand it.

exploration (ek spluh RAY shuhn) *noun*   When you do an **exploration**, you look at something carefully to learn about it.

experience (ik SPIR ee uhns) *noun*   An **experience** is an event that you have lived through.

express (ik SPRES) *verb*   When you **express** an idea or a feeling, you put it into words, pictures, or actions.

F

factor (FAK tuhr) *noun*   A **factor** is a cause or happening that helps bring about a result.

factual (FAK chuh wuhl) *adjective*   Something that is **factual** is true or real.

fantasy (FAN tuh see) *noun*   A **fantasy** is something that is unreal or imagined.

feedback (FEED bak) *noun*   When you give **feedback**, you tell or show your response to something.

G

generalization (jen ruh luh ZAY shuhn) *noun*   A **generalization** is a statement, rule, or principle that applies to many people or things.

global (GLOH buhl) *adjective*   Something that is **global** involves the whole world.

I

identify (y DEN tuh fy) *verb*   When you **identify** something, you tell what it is or who owns it.

illogical (il LAH ji kuhl) *adjective*   Something that goes against what is reasonable or expected is **illogical**.

imitate (I muh tayt) *verb*   When you **imitate** someone or something, you try to be like the person or thing.

individuality (in duh vi juh WA luh tee) *noun*   **Individuality** is all the qualities that make one person or thing different from another.

inequality (i ni KWAH luh tee) *noun*   **Inequality** exists when people are not treated the same or given the same rights.

influence (IN floo uhns) *noun*   **Influence** is the effect that something has on a person or thing.

influence (IN floo uhns) *verb*   To **influence** people is to have an effect on their actions or thoughts.

inform (in FAWRM) *verb*   When you **inform** someone of something, you give the person knowledge of it.

injury (INJ ree) *noun*   An **injury** is harm or damage done to someone or something.

insecurity (in si KYOOR uh tee) *noun*   **Insecurity** refers to a lack of confidence.

interact (in tuhr AKT) *verb*   When you **interact** with people, you exchange information with them.

introduce (in truh DOOS) *verb*   You **introduce** something when you bring it to a place, or cause it to be used, for the first time.

invariably (in VER ee uh blee) *adverb*   An event or a situation that happens **invariably** always happens.

investigate (in VES tuh gayt) *verb*   To **investigate** something is to look at it carefully to find out the truth.

irritate (IR uh tayt) *verb*   When you **irritate** someone, you annoy or anger the person.

J

judge (juhj) *verb*   When you **judge** someone or something, you form an opinion about the person or thing.

L

literal (LI tuh ruhl) *adjective*   Things that are **literal** stick to the facts or follow the exact meaning of words.

locate (LOH kayt) *verb*   When you **locate** an object, you find where it is.

M

meaningful (MEE ning fuhl) *adjective*
When something is **meaningful**, it is important and filled with significance and purpose.

measure (ME zhuhr) *verb*   When you **measure** something, you figure out its size.

media (MEE dee uh) *noun*   The **media** are radio, television, the Internet, newspapers, and all other forms of communication that reach large audiences.

method (ME thuhd) *noun*   A **method** is a way of doing something.

mislead (mis LEED) *verb*   When you **mislead** people, you give them the wrong idea about something.

misunderstand (mi suhn duhr STAND) *verb*   When you **misunderstand** someone, you get the wrong idea about what the person meant.

N

negotiate (ni GOH shee ayt) *verb*   To **negotiate** with someone is to try to reach an agreement through discussion and compromise.

O

objective (uhb JEK tiv) *adjective*
When you are **objective**, you try to separate your feelings about something from the facts.

observe (uhb ZUHRV) *verb*   To **observe** is to look at something carefully or to study it.

observation (ahb suhr VAY shuhn) *noun*   An **observation** is something you witness or a comment you make about what you have seen.

occur (uh KUHR) *verb*   To **occur** is to happen.

opinion (uh PIN yuhn) *verb*   An **opinion** is the way you think or feel about something, which may or may not be based on facts.

oppose (uh POHZ) *verb*   When you **oppose** something, you take a position against it.

outdated (owt DAY tuhd) *adjective*   When something is **outdated**, it is old-fashioned or no longer in use.

overcome (oh vuhr KUHM) *verb*   To **overcome** something is to beat it or conquer it.

P

persuade (puhr SWAYD) *verb*   To **persuade** is to convince someone to think or act a certain way.

point (poynt) *noun*   A **point** is an important idea or fact.

probable (PRAH buh buhl) *adjective* When something is **probable**, it is likely to happen.

process (PRAH ses) *noun*   A **process** is a set of steps you follow to complete an action.

prove (proov) *verb*   When you **prove** something, you show that it is true or correct.

Q

quality (KWAH luh tee) *noun*   The **quality** of something is how good it is.

quantity (KWAHN tuh tee) *noun* A **quantity** is an amount.

R

reaction (ree AK shuhn) *noun* A **reaction** to something is the feeling it causes or the action taken in response.

relevant (RE luh vuhnt) *adjective* When something is **relevant** to a topic, it helps make a point about the topic.

represent (re pri ZENT) *verb*   To **represent** is to stand for someone or something.

respond (ri SPAHND) *verb*   When you **respond** to something, you react or answer back.

reveal (ri VEEL) *verb*   When you show something that has been hidden, you **reveal** it.

S

sensory (SENS ree) *adjective*   Something that is **sensory** has to do with one or more of the five senses.

separate (SE puh rayt) *verb*   When you **separate** things or people, you keep them apart.

signal (SIG nuhl) *noun*   A **signal** is a sign of something to come.

significance (sig NI fi kuhns) *noun* The **significance** of something is the thing that makes it important or meaningful.

solution (suh LOO shuhn) *noun* A **solution** is an answer to a problem.

stalemate (STAYL mayt) *noun* A **stalemate** is a situation in which no further action can occur.

statistics (stuh TIS tiks) *noun*   **Statistics** are facts presented in the form of numbers.

substitute (SUHB stuh toot) *noun*
A **substitute** is something or someone that takes the place of another.

suffering (SUH fuh ring) *noun*
Suffering is being in a lot of pain or distress.

superficial (soo puhr FI shuhl) *adjective* When you do things in a **superficial** way, you do them quickly and without much thought.

symbolize (SIM buh lyz) *verb* When things represent or stand for something else, they **symbolize** it.

sympathy (SIM puh thee) *noun*
When you have **sympathy** for someone, you understand and share the person's feelings.

T

theory (THEE uh ree) *noun* A **theory** is a central idea on which you base an argument.

tolerance (TAH luh ruhns) *noun*
Tolerance is letting other people have their own beliefs, even if their beliefs differ from yours.

U

unify (YOO nuh fy) *verb* When you **unify** people or things, you bring them together.

V

valid (VA luhd) *adjective* To be **valid** is to be based on truth or on fact.

valuable (VAL yuh buhl) *adjective*
Something that is **valuable** is worth a lot.

variation (ver ee AY shuhn) *noun*
A **variation** is a change or difference from the usual pattern.

victorious (vik TOHR ee uhs) *adjective*
A **victorious** person has won something, such as a contest or a race.

viewpoint (VYOO poynt) *noun* A **viewpoint** is the way a person looks at or thinks about something.

violence (VY luhns) *noun* **Violence** is the use of physical force to harm someone or to damage property.

INDEX

Use the index to find out more about real-life topics.

Illustrations

Gary Hathaway 2-3, 38-39, 74-75, 110-111, 146-147, 166-167.

Maps

XNR Productions, Inc.: 62.

Photographs

Every effort has been made to secure permission and provide appropriate credit for photographic material. The publisher deeply regrets any omission and pledges to correct errors called to its attention in subsequent editions.

Unless otherwise acknowledged, all photographs are the property of Pearson Education, Inc.

Photo locators denoted as follows: Top (T), Center (C), Bottom (B), Left (L), Right (R), Background (Bkgd)

COVER (Bkgd T) Hisham Ibrahim/Getty Images, (Bkgd TR) Getty Images, (Bkgd L) Nic Miller/Organics Image Library/Alamy, (Bkgd C & B) Alvis Upitis/Getty Images, (L) Purestock/Getty Images, (C) Nancy Ney/Getty Images, (R) Jupiter Images; 5 Brad Killer/iStockphoto; 6 Pornchai Kittiwongsakul/Getty Images; 9 Jack/ Dagley Photography/Shutterstock; 13 Peter Leyden/iStockphoto; 14 Matt Rourke/AP Images; 17 Hannamariah/Shutterstock; 21 Izabela Habur/iStockphoto; 25 Nuno Silva/iStockphoto; 29 Chris Schmidt/ iStockphoto; 33 moodboard/Punchstock; 41 Roman Kobzarev/iStockphoto; 45 Vincent Giordano/Shutterstock; 49 Ravi Tahilramani/ iStockphoto; 53 Trista Weibell/iStockphoto; 61 Dana Bartekoske/Shutterstock; 62 (B) Shutterstock, (T) Shutterstock; 65 Sami Suni/ iStockphoto; 70 Jeff Greenberg/PhotoEdit; 77 Bill Grove/iStockphoto; 81 National Archives; 85 Clara Natoli/Shutterstock; 86 Mario Savoia/Shutterstock; 89 Tony Barson/WireImage/Getty Images; 93 David H. Lewis/iStockphoto; 94 Dar Yang Yan/ iStockphoto; 97 David Frazier/PhotoEdit; 101 Jeff Greenberg/PhotoEdit; 105 Rebecca Ellis/iStockphoto; 106 steba/Shutterstock; 113 Michael Ochs Archives/Getty Images; 117 Jason Stitt/iStockphoto; 121 Jeremy Edwards/iStockphoto; 125 Carson Walker/ AP Images; 126 Richard Gunion/iStockphoto; 129 Shutterstock; 133 Shutterstock; 137 Jaimie Duplass/iStockphoto; 138 Larry Goren/Icon SMI/Corbis; 141 Laurence Gough/ iStockphoto; 142 Chris Schmidt/iStockphoto; 149 Jani Bryson/iStockphoto; 157 Jason R. Warren/iStockphoto; 158 Ed Betz/AP Images; 161 Margaret Bourke-White/Stringer/Getty Images; 169 Al Behrman/AP Images; 170 Shutterstock; 173 Sean Martin/ iStockphoto; 181 Anne Frank Fonds - Basel/Anne Frank House/Getty Images; 177 iStockphoto; 178 visitbemidji; 185 David Mager/Arena-PAL Images; 189 Joe Rosenthal/ AP Images; 192 Shutterstock; 193 William Lovelace/Stringer/Getty Images; 194 Bettmann/Corbis; 197 Daniel Bendjy/ iStockphoto.